3 1994 01101 8030

SANTA ANA PUBLIC LIBRARY
NEWHOPE BRANCH

D1022133

WOMEN IN
MEDICINE

PROFILES

Amazing Archaeologists and Their Finds
America's Most Influential First Ladies
America's Third-Party Presidential Candidates
Black Abolitionists and Freedom Fighters
Black Civil Rights Champions
Charismatic Cult Leaders
Courageous Crimefighters
Environmental Pioneers
Great Auto Makers and Their Cars
Great Justices of the Supreme Court
Hatemongers and Demagogues
Hoaxers and Hustlers
International Terrorists
Journalists Who Made History
Legendary Labor Leaders
Philanthropists and Their Legacies
Soviet Leaders from Lenin to Gorbachev
Top Entrepreneurs and Their Businesses
Top Lawyers and Their Famous Cases
Treacherous Traitors
Utopian Visionaries
Women Business Leaders
Women Chosen for Public Office
Women in Medicine
Women Inventors and Their Discoveries
Women of the U.S. Congress
Women Who Led Nations
Women Who Reformed Politics
The World's Greatest Explorers

WOMEN IN MEDICINE

Jacqueline C. Kent

J 920 KEN
Kent, Jacqueline C.
Women in medicine

                                    $19.96
NEWHOPE   31994011018030

The Oliver Press, Inc.
Minneapolis

The publisher would like to thank Charlotte Bell, M.D., Department of Anesthesiology, Yale University School of Medicine, for her review of this book.

The publisher also wishes to thank Vicki Thomson, M.D., Edina Pediatrics, Edina, Minnesota, for her participation in this book.

Copyright © 1998 by The Oliver Press, Inc.
All rights reserved.
No part of this book may be reproduced in any form or by any means without permission in writing from the publisher.
Please address inquiries to:

The Oliver Press, Inc.
Charlotte Square
5707 West 36th Street
Minneapolis, MN 55416-2510

Library of Congress Cataloging-in-Publication Data

Kent, Jacqueline C.
Women in medicine / Jacqueline C. Kent
p.   cm.—(Profiles)
Includes bibliographical references and index.
    Summary: Profiles eight women who broke gender, racial, and other barriers to become doctors.
ISBN 1-881508-46-3 (lib. bdg.)
1. Women in medicine—United States—Biography—Juvenile literature. [1. Women in medicine. 2. Physicians. 3. Women—Biography.] I. Title. II. Series: Profiles (Minneapolis, Minn.)
R692.K46 1998
610'.82'0973—dc21
[B]   97-30235
                                          CIP
                                           AC

ISBN 1-881508-46-3
Printed in the United States of America

04 03 02 01 00 99 98   8 7 6 5 4 3 2 1

Contents

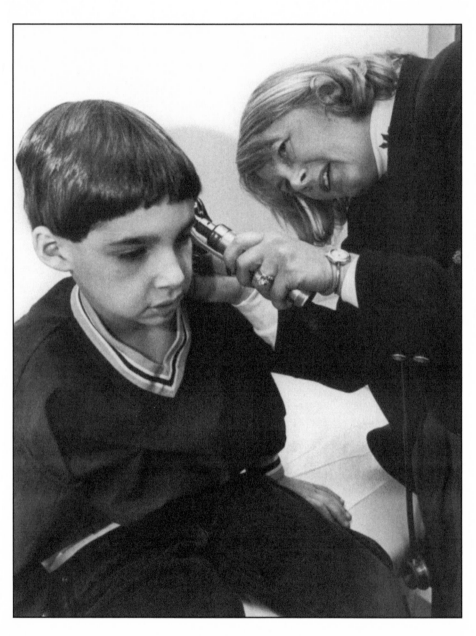

As late as 1970, women made up less than 8 percent of all physicians in the United States. It is estimated that by the year 2010 that number will reach 30 percent.

Introduction

*T*oday, you can walk into any clinic or hospital and see female doctors at work. While this does not seem unusual now, women were denied the opportunity to serve as physicians or surgeons not long ago. Only through the efforts of generations of women who fought for the right to be called "Doctor" are today's women free to take up the practice of medicine. The eight female physicians profiled in this book were leaders in that struggle.

When Elizabeth Blackwell enrolled in New York's Geneva College of Medicine in 1847, the idea of women studying medicine shocked and outraged many people. Everyone knew that medicine was a man's profession—everyone, that is, but Blackwell herself and her few supporters. She withstood opposition from the male doctors who dominated the medical profession and became the first woman to earn a medical degree in the United States.

Blackwell was not, of course, the first woman to help those who were ill. For centuries, women had cared for their sick family members, learning to heal by trial and error and passing on their knowledge. Often they came to the aid of others in their communities, particularly other women. During some time periods and in some places, the public accepted female healers. In other times and places, women were banned from practicing medicine.

Elizabeth Blackwell had searched through historical records for evidence of other women who shared her interest in medicine. What she found amazed her. She learned that during Queen Hatshepsut's reign in Egypt (about 1490 to 1470 B.C.), women as well as men attended medical school. Blackwell also discovered that a drawing on the tomb of Egyptian Pharaoh Ramses II, who had died 200 years after the end of Queen Hatshepsut's rule, depicted a female surgeon at work.

Blackwell read that the wife and daughter of the famous Greek mathematician Pythagoras had been healers in the sixth century B.C. and that women had attended medical schools started by Hippocrates, a Greek physician who lived from approximately 460 to 377 B.C. Blackwell also studied the list of female medical practitioners compiled by Claudius Galen, a Greek-born physician who had practiced in Rome during the second century. He, apparently, had shared her interest in women doctors.

Doctors today still recite the Hippocratic Oath, which states the ethical principles of Hippocrates (left). The medical findings of Galen (A.D. 130-201) were considered so brilliant that little new research was performed until the sixteenth century.

Blackwell discovered that women doctors had even served kings and queens. One woman, Hersend, was the physician accompanying King Louis IX of France when he went to the Middle East in about A.D. 1250. And Queen Philippa, the wife of England's King Edward III, hired Cecilia of Oxford as her surgeon in the mid-1300s.

From the earliest days of humanity, female friends and family members assisted women during childbirth. *Midwives* were women who were expert in childbearing. An experienced midwife could tell whether the baby was positioned correctly for birth, and she knew what to do if complications arose. When no priests were available, some European midwives during the Middle Ages (around A.D. 500-1500) even baptized infants whose survival looked questionable.

Centuries later, midwives in the North American colonies earned the respect of those they helped in their communities. In addition to delivering babies, some of these women treated injuries and illnesses and became known as "doctresses." During colonial times, both men and women acquired their skills by working with experienced medical practitioners in apprenticeships that usually lasted about seven years. Only as the requirements to practice medicine became more structured did the acceptance of women medical practitioners decline.

This change in the medical profession began in the colonies during the mid-eighteenth century, when American men started traveling to Europe for rigorous medical training at universities. (Except for a few exceptional cases, women were not allowed to study in European institutions until Switzerland's University of Zurich allowed women to enroll in 1865.) Some of these American physicians later established America's first medical school in Philadelphia, Pennsylvania, in 1765.

In order to raise the standards of their profession, America's new medical-school graduates began to require prospective doctors to become licensed and pass exams that tested their knowledge. Unfortunately, the medical programs were closed to women, so they could not even take the exams. As more men gained licenses to practice medicine, women healers began to lose acceptance in their communities.

By the latter half of the eighteenth century, male physicians had taken charge of all areas of medicine except for midwifery and nursing. Then, as medical-school students learned more about the body through the study of anatomy, even the domain of midwifery was invaded by male physicians. Middle-class and wealthy women assumed that because of their years of schooling men could deliver babies more safely than less educated midwives. Pregnant women began choosing men with medical degrees to deliver their babies.

Only in the mid-nineteenth century did American medical schools grudgingly allow women the formal education they needed to become licensed doctors. Geneva College of Medicine allowed Elizabeth Blackwell to become the first woman to enroll in its program in 1847. Soon after Blackwell's admission, medical schools exclusively for women began to be established. In 1848, health reformer Samuel Gregory joined with American feminists to establish the New England Female Medical College in Boston. Then, in 1850, the Female (later Woman's) Medical College of Pennsylvania opened.

Still, graduates from these women-only schools were often perceived by the great majority of their male colleagues as having received a substandard education. In addition, the most prestigious medical schools in the United States remained closed to women. So many

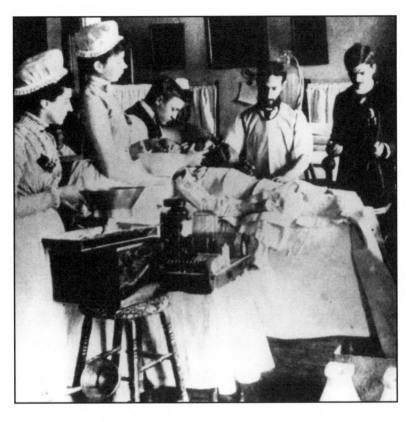

As shown in this photograph from the mid-1880s, women's participation in nineteenth-century medicine was still largely confined to the profession of nursing.

women continued to fight for entrance into schools that were *coeducational*, teaching men and women together. Even after Blackwell's success, women found it difficult to find a good school that would accept them. Blackwell's younger sister, Emily, was turned down by 11 schools before finally gaining admittance into Chicago's Rush Medical School. She studied there only one year before the Illinois State Medical Society forced Rush to bar her from further study.

A significant breakthrough occurred in 1893 when the new Johns Hopkins Medical School in Baltimore, Maryland, opened its doors to women. This remarkable event happened because three wealthy women agreed to provide $500,000 for the construction of the medical school—but only if the institution allowed women to enroll. In order to receive the necessary funding, the board of directors agreed to these terms, and 3 of the 21 students entering the medical school its first semester were women. By the end of the nineteenth century, 1,500 female students—10 percent of the total enrollment—were studying in America's medical schools.

Although they were gaining ground, women still faced many obstacles. One was the denial of *internship* opportunities. As part of their education, medical students were required to work directly with patients under the supervision of experienced doctors. This training allowed them to apply their studies to actual cases. By the beginning of the 1920s, only eight percent of U.S. hospitals accepted female interns. Since internships were vital to obtaining a medical license, even women with medical degrees had difficulty becoming doctors.

Opportunities for female doctors expanded temporarily when the United States entered World War II in 1941. With American men donning uniforms and heading off to battle, there was suddenly a shortage of male

Many medical schools still barred women long after Elizabeth Blackwell graduated from Geneva in 1849. Harvard Medical School, shown here, did not allow women to earn medical degrees until 1945.

medical students. Rather than face empty classrooms, some medical schools began accepting more women.

When the war ended in 1945, however, medical schools no longer needed female students. As a result, the number of women accepted into medical programs dropped. Women's entrance into medical schools in the United States would not grow significantly until after 1970, when congressional hearings revealed that some medical schools had designed their admissions policies to keep women out of the medical profession. These hearings led the Women's Equity Action League (WEAL) to file a complaint against every single medical school in the country. After this successful legal battle, female enrollment jumped from 9 percent of all medical students in 1970 to more than 40 percent in 1994.

Like Elizabeth Blackwell, the other women profiled in this book faced barriers in their quest to become doctors. During the American Civil War (1861-1865), Mary Edwards Walker fought for the right to perform surgery on Union troops. Seventy years later, Virginia Apgar was forced to give up her dream of becoming a surgeon because most people in the 1930s still were afraid to trust female surgeons. Fortunately, Apgar persevered in another branch of medicine and later developed a delivery-room procedure now used worldwide to analyze the condition of newborns immediately after birth. Alma Dea Morani overcame similar discrimination to become the first female plastic surgeon.

In addition to facing obstacles because of their gender, some women physicians also struggled with racial discrimination. When May Edward Chinn, the daughter of a former slave, graduated from medical school in 1926, many hospitals still refused to hire African Americans. Black physicians often had to find alternative ways to take care of their patients. Chinn, for example, sometimes performed surgery in a patient's home using an ironing board as her operating table!

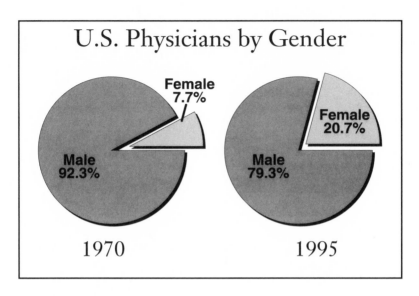

U.S. Physicians by Gender

Female
7.7%

Male
92.3%

1970

Female
20.7%

Male
79.3%

1995

These charts show that the number of women doctors in the U.S. substantially increased after 1970.

Some of the women profiled in this book also met other challenges that threatened to steal their dreams. Blackwell lost her vision in one eye. Helen Brooke Taussig, who developed a medical procedure that to this day continues to save the lives of "blue babies," battled dyslexia and hearing loss. Susan La Flesche Picotte, the first American Indian woman to earn a degree in medicine, endured painful headaches and a debilitating bone infection. And Dorothy Lavinia Brown, who experienced the loneliness of being raised in an orphanage, became the first black female surgeon in the South.

Medicine has evolved dramatically since the mid-nineteenth century when Elizabeth Blackwell first applied

16

to medical school. The field now encompasses specialties and subspecialties that would have surprised Blackwell and her contemporaries. But the most welcome change is that women no longer have to fight for the right to become doctors. They do not sit apart from the male students in classrooms; nor are women barred from certain lectures because they are considered too "delicate" for the subject matter. They are accepted into medical programs all over the country and may apply for internships at any institution. In fact, in 1997, the American Medical Association, the nation's largest organization of doctors, elected Dr. Nancy Dickey as its first female president. The eight women in this book can claim a great share of the credit for this progress.

Dr. Nancy W. Dickey, a family physician from College Station, Texas, was elected president of the American Medical Association in June 1997.

*The first woman in the United States to earn a
medical degree, Elizabeth Blackwell (1821-1910)
depended upon her formidable self-discipline. As a
child, she had sometimes even slept on the floor to
"harden" her body.*

1

Elizabeth Blackwell
First Among Equals

*Y*oung Elizabeth crawled wearily into the dark closet and shut the door behind her. Drawing herself into a ball, she fought to control the shivers caused by her fever. It had gripped her for days, first giving her chills and then sweats. She tried to "walk it off," but her legs quickly tired and buckled under the physical strain. So now she found the quietest place in the house and curled up, determined to overcome the fever.

When Aunt Bar found Elizabeth huddled in the closet, she packed her off to bed, not at all surprised that the child would try to force her body to cure itself. Elizabeth's quiet strength had been apparent almost from the moment of her birth. During the first few days of her life, the family was not sure she would survive, but little Elizabeth endured. Later she even outran and outclimbed her brothers. Indeed, Elizabeth developed a self-discipline and inner strength that would remain with her into adulthood and sustain her through the trying years of her pioneering career in medicine.

The Blackwell family was a large one—Elizabeth was the third of nine surviving children. Her life began on February 3, 1821, in a town called Counterslip in England. She and her sisters were fortunate because their father, unlike many adults in the early 1800s, believed that boys and girls should be educated together. Private tutors taught the Blackwell children, and the girls studied the same subjects as the boys.

Elizabeth's father, Samuel Blackwell, was a prosperous sugar refiner and a deeply religious man. Her mother, Hannah, had grown up in a cultured family environment and was used to luxurious surroundings, elegant dinner parties, and all the other privileges of an affluent lifestyle. Although she respected her husband's desire for a simple Christian life, she still managed to introduce her children to good books and fine music.

Elizabeth was only 11 when her father's sugar refinery burned to the ground. After much prayer, Samuel decided to move his large family from England to the

Like these immigrants arriving at New York's Castle Garden in the early nineteenth century, Samuel Blackwell and his family moved to the United States for a better life. "You children will have more opportunities there," he declared.

United States in the summer of 1832. They settled in New York City, where Samuel opened another sugar refinery. But the business did not thrive, and the family moved twice more before settling in Cincinnati, Ohio, in 1838. Shortly after this move, Samuel Blackwell died, leaving the family almost penniless.

Elizabeth would remember her father's death as "an irreparable loss" that "completely altered our lives." To

21

earn money to support the family, she and her two older sisters opened a private school in their home. Later, Elizabeth spent a year teaching in Henderson, Kentucky. There she witnessed slavery for the first time. It disgusted her. Her revulsion with life in the South, coupled with a growing restlessness and desire to do something other than teaching, led her to return to Cincinnati.

While Elizabeth was grappling with her career decisions, she had an experience that changed her life. One of

Samuel Blackwell had taught his children to despise the buying and selling of human beings, as in this slave auction. Elizabeth's hatred of slavery grew when she saw firsthand the squalid conditions and brutal treatment of slaves living in Kentucky.

her friends was dying. As the ill woman lay in her deathbed, she confided to Elizabeth that her suffering would have been lessened had there been a female physician to attend her. The embarrassment of being examined by a male doctor had made a bad situation even worse. The dying friend thought Elizabeth would make a fine doctor, and she encouraged the young woman to think about studying medicine.

Initially, Elizabeth did not take her friend's suggestion seriously. "I hated everything connected with the body," she remembered. Elizabeth could not even "bear the sight of a medical book." As a young student, she had been forced to view a surgically removed cow's eye during a science class demonstration, and she recalled her horror. How could she study medicine and become a doctor, Elizabeth wondered, if the sight of body parts upset her so much?

But even though Elizabeth tried to ignore the woman's advice, she could not deny that she yearned for a challenge. All around her, strong women were stepping out of their homes to agitate passionately for important causes. Some worked for the abolition of slavery, while others spoke out against alcohol abuse. Many women demanded freedoms such as dress reform, improvements in education, and especially the right to vote. Elizabeth realized that if she studied medicine, perhaps she could open the door for other women who might be dreaming of becoming doctors.

Formidable barriers stood in her path, however. Although women had been nurses for years and midwives for centuries, medical schools in the United States were exclusively for male students. Nevertheless, Elizabeth remained undaunted. "It was to my mind a moral crusade in which I had entered," she explained. And she would allow nothing to disrupt her quest.

Elizabeth began to investigate how she might study medicine. She wrote to physicians—all men—who were friends of her family. Although they felt she would make a good doctor, their responses were not very encouraging. One even suggested that she dress up as a man to attend classes! In spite of their discouraging words, Elizabeth vowed to find a way to study medicine.

Her first challenge was money. The little money her family possessed barely covered their living expenses, so Elizabeth knew she would have to support herself during her schooling. For two years, she taught school in North and South Carolina and saved her earnings. She also began studying medicine on her own by borrowing books from the libraries of physicians with whom she was acquainted.

By 1847, Blackwell had saved enough money to begin her search for a medical school. But every medical school she applied to in Philadelphia and New York City turned her down. Not easily discouraged, Elizabeth kept trying. Finally, Geneva College of Medicine in Geneva, New York, accepted her in October 1847. Ironically, her

Founded in 1834, Geneva College of Medicine was moved to Syracuse to become part of Syracuse University in 1875. Since 1950, the school has been the State University of New York Health Science Center.

acceptance came about as a result of a misunderstanding. The professors had left the decision of admitting Elizabeth up to the student body. The students, assuming that a rival school was playing a prank on them, voted to admit her, much to their professors' surprise.

Acceptance into medical school was an important step for Elizabeth, but she still faced other obstacles. When she entered a medical-school classroom for the first time, for instance, she was greeted with complete silence from the stunned students. She sat down and tried her best to listen to the instructor's lecture while her male classmates gawked at her. Over time, she learned to endure paper notes tossed into her lap and bumps and pokes from the other students.

On one occasion, a professor asked her not to attend a classroom demonstration on anatomy because he considered it too "indelicate" for a woman. She responded by promising to sit quietly and to remove her bonnet if it distracted him. Impressed by her attitude, the professor allowed her to view the demonstration, and the subject never came up again. Gradually she won the respect of most of her classmates as well. Several students from her anatomy class even invited Elizabeth to participate in their study group.

The townspeople were harder to win over. Many residents of the town avoided her. They assumed that any woman who wanted to attend medical school, surrounded by men, had to be either promiscuous or simply crazy. Every evening Elizabeth walked home alone, ignoring the rude stares that followed her, and shut herself inside the bare room she rented.

During the summer break of 1848, Elizabeth worked at the Blockley Almshouse, a hospital for poor immigrants in Philadelphia. It was a good chance to observe the practice of medicine close up, but serving at Blockley also gave Elizabeth a taste of the prejudice she would face once she had her medical degree. The male

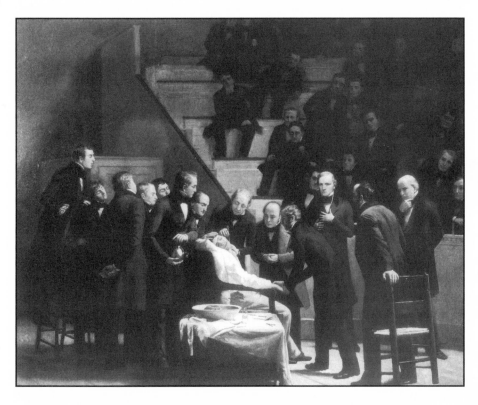

As shown in this painting of the first surgery using anesthesia, which was performed in October 1846, men dominated the field of medicine in Blackwell's day.

students' behavior at Geneva paled in comparison to what she suffered at Blockley, where male colleagues completely refused to associate with her. When she walked into a ward to visit patients, the male doctors promptly disappeared. And whenever Elizabeth was on duty, the physicians refused to write the required information about patients' illnesses on their bedside charts, leaving her to diagnose their problems by herself.

In spite of the doctors' rudeness, Blockley proved a valuable training ground for Elizabeth. While she worked there, an epidemic engulfed Ireland, and huge numbers of Irish immigrants arrived in the United States burning with fever. Blockley housed so many of them that many patients had to sleep on the floor. To make the conditions worse, the doctors at Blockley paid little attention to the cleanliness of either the ward or the patients.

Stepping over the sick strewn about Blockley's ward, Elizabeth began to see the importance of hygiene in preventing illness. The doctors and nurses, she thought, should wash their hands and make sure their patients were kept clean. The patients' clothing and bed linens should be frequently laundered. Elizabeth later wrote about her experience with the epidemic in a research paper on hygiene that she was required to complete for her medical degree.

In autumn 1848, Elizabeth returned to New York and her studies. After her trials at Blockley, Geneva seemed almost like returning home. As the time for graduation approached, her professors began to worry about the reaction of the public and the medical community if they awarded Elizabeth a medical degree. But when the final tally of grades revealed that hers were the highest in her class, they knew they could not refuse Elizabeth a diploma. On January 23, 1849, Elizabeth Blackwell graduated with honors. She was the first woman to earn a medical degree in the United States.

Doctor Blackwell had worked hard to obtain her degree, so a short rest would have been perfectly justified. But she was anxious to move on to the greater challenge of becoming a surgeon. She realized, however, that there were limited opportunities for women to study in the United States. So, at the invitation of one of her cousins, Elizabeth traveled to England, where she visited hospitals and attended lectures. Then she went to Paris, France, for additional training. While in Paris, she enrolled in a midwife's course to gain practical experience delivering babies.

It was in Paris that Dr. Blackwell's dream of becoming a surgeon ended abruptly. One evening, Blackwell was using a syringe to squirt water into the eye of a child with an infection called ophthalmia. She accidentally splashed some tainted water into her own eye and quickly contracted the horrible infection. Even though she received the best treatment available, she lost her sight in her left eye. Blackwell was devastated. But despite her vision loss, she decided to continue her study of medicine.

In October 1850, Blackwell returned to London, England. There she worked and studied under the guidance of Dr. James Paget at St. Bartholomew's Hospital. Paget allowed her to accompany the medical specialists as they walked through the hospital wards, examining patients and making decisions about treatments. She conversed with doctors who were specialists in a number of fields. One doctor's specialty was *lateral lithotomy*, an

While in London, Blackwell studied under Sir James Paget (1814-1899), one of the founders of modern pathology—*the study of the nature and origin of disease. In 1834, Paget had discovered that the disease* trichinosis *was caused by eating undercooked pork.*

operation to remove stones from the bladder. Another was researching *dysentery*, a life-threatening disease that infected the bowels and caused terrible diarrhea.

During this time, Blackwell befriended a woman named Florence Nightingale, who within a few years would become famous for her revolutionary work as a nurse during the Crimean War (1853-1856) in Russia. Nightingale and Blackwell stayed in contact throughout the rest of their lives, encouraging each other in their groundbreaking careers.

Blackwell met Florence Nightingale while studying in London. Nightingale (1820-1910), the founder of modern nursing, became a legend while caring for sick and wounded soldiers during the Crimean War.

As the year 1851 passed its midpoint, Blackwell recrossed the Atlantic Ocean to return to the United States, eager to begin her career. But no hospital or clinic would hire her. In fact, no one would even rent her office space for her practice. Ignoring this setback, Blackwell found another way to use her medical expertise. She continued to explore her interest in hygiene by writing and presenting a series of lectures explaining the importance of regular bathing and keeping bathrooms and kitchens clean. A clean home, she stressed, would lead to improved health. In 1852, New York City publisher G. P. Putnam published her lectures as *The Laws of Life, with Special Reference to the Physical Education of Girls.*

Blackwell's lectures proved helpful in another way. A group of prominent women from the Society of Friends, or Quakers, attended her talks and were so impressed that they used their influence to help the young doctor. They encouraged one Quaker family to engage Blackwell as its physician, and gradually she was allowed to make more house calls to other Quaker patients.

Dr. Blackwell still hoped, however, to work in a clinic, where the number of patients and the variety of illnesses she could treat daily would be greater than in this kind of private practice. No clinics would hire her, so she decided to open her own. "With the aid of some of my friends," Blackwell recalled, "a small room was engaged in a poor quarter of the town." Her tiny clinic served needy patients for the next two years. Despite the constant opposition of her neighbors, the doctor eventually was able to purchase a house and expand her clinic.

Although Blackwell now kept busy, she was still lonely. Her family had moved to England and she knew few other doctors. To help fill the void in her life, she adopted a young child named Katharine in 1854. Proof that Blackwell's efforts were beginning to influence young women could be observed in her own daughter. When "Kitty" met a male doctor for the first time, she declared how "very odd it is to hear a *man* called Doctor!"

Nor was Dr. Blackwell alone at her clinic for long. Her younger sister, Emily, graduated from medical school in 1854 and soon joined her. Blackwell's staff increased to three when Dr. Maria E. Zakrzewska came aboard a short

Dr. Marie Zakrzewska (1829-1902), who had emigrated from Poland in 1853, met Blackwell the following year. Blackwell helped her new friend master English and invited the talented physician to join her clinic in 1856.

time later. Overjoyed at being able to work together, the three doctors made plans to accomplish another of Blackwell's goals—the establishment of a hospital in which women physicians could train in internships. Even though some medical schools now admitted women, opportunities for internships in hospitals were still rare. As a result, women doctors suffered from inadequate on-the-job training.

To set up a hospital required money, so the three partners embarked on a round of fundraising. Finally, they acquired the necessary funds. In 1857, the women expanded their clinic into the New York Infirmary for Women and Children—the first hospital in the world run by female doctors.

When the Civil War erupted four years later, Dr. Blackwell called her hospital's managers together to discuss how they could help the Union's war effort. Two organizations emerged from their meetings: the Women's Central Association of Relief and the U.S. Sanitary Commission. Through these groups, Blackwell selected and trained nurses for war service. Women from all over the United States sent in applications for nursing positions. After training, the new nurses served wherever they were needed by Union forces.

Following the war's end in 1865, Dr. Blackwell continued to raise educational standards for female medical students. She added the Woman's Medical College to her hospital in 1868 and broke new ground by requiring

The New York Infirmary for Women and Children, the first hospital in the world directed by women, was founded by Blackwell, her sister Emily Blackwell, and Marie Zakrzewska in May 1857.

entrance examinations a decade before they were man-dated by state law. In addition, she created a three-year course of study with longer terms than at other medical schools. Next, recalling her own difficulties during med-ical training, Blackwell made sure that her students received adequate hands-on clinical experience. Finally, to avoid any question of special privileges to help the women graduate, Blackwell set up an examining board that was independent of the school. The examiners held the students to the highest standards.

By 1869, feeling she could do no more for women's medical education in the United States, Blackwell again turned her attention across the Atlantic. Always interested in involving her home country in her work, she had traveled to England a decade earlier to lecture and meet with women who were interested in the medical profession. In 1869, she returned to England, leaving the Woman's Medical College in her sister's capable hands.

Blackwell established a large practice in London and rekindled her old interest in hygiene. To this end, she helped organize the National Health Society in 1871. Following the society's motto, "Prevention is better than cure," Blackwell hoped to educate people about the importance of hygiene and sanitation and to teach them how polluted water supplies and unclean living conditions could harm their families' health.

In 1875, Dr. Blackwell accepted a position as professor of gynecology at the London School of Medicine for Women. Although poor health forced her to give up her professorship a year later, Blackwell continued to write. Over the course of the next 30 years, she published two books and many articles, often addressing the issues of sex education and sexual morality in a forthright manner shocking to her contemporaries. In her work, Blackwell always stressed the "special and weighty responsibility" that all doctors—both men and women—shared.

They should take great pains, she wrote, "to see that human beings are well born, well nourished, and well educated." She lived according to this belief her whole life.

While visiting a favorite inn during the summer of 1907, Blackwell slipped and fell down a flight of stairs. She never completely recovered from the injury and eventually died in Hastings, England, on May 31, 1910, at the age of 89.

Despite the hardships she had endured in pursuit of her dream, including the loss of sight in one eye, Dr. Elizabeth Blackwell paved the way for generations of women who would follow her. She had boldly stepped into a career field long considered a male domain and had found success. Because of her pioneering efforts, countless women have pursued fulfilling careers and have made valuable contributions to the field of medicine. When Blackwell received her degree from the hand of Geneva Medical College's president in 1849, she promised him to make it "the effort of my life to shed honor upon your diploma." Her years as a doctor did just that.

Dr. Mary Walker (1832-1919) poses in the men's attire that she preferred to the elaborate dresses most women wore at the time. Note the Congressional Medal of Honor pinned to her lapel, which she won for bravery as a surgeon during the Civil War.

2

Mary Edwards Walker
The Union's Rebel Surgeon

*R*everend Samuel J. May stood ready to perform the marriage service while Dr. Albert Miller, the groom, paced nervously nearby. The guests inside the farmhouse whispered among themselves, anxious to view the bride in her wedding finery. When she finally appeared, the guests were stunned. Mary Edwards Walker stood before them, neatly clad in trousers and a dress coat!

Walker knew her choice of attire would startle her guests, but she believed the dresses worn by her contemporaries, with their heavy layers and viselike corsets, harmed women physically. Her choice of clothing reflected her willingness to act on her convictions, even if others criticized and ridiculed her. This attitude guided the choices Mary Walker made and the causes she championed throughout her life. In addition to fighting for dress reform, Walker chose a medical career at a time when few women did so, eventually becoming the first female surgeon in the U.S. Army. For her efforts, Mary often faced hostility and derision, but she never abandoned her beliefs.

Mary Edwards Walker was born to Alvah and Vesta Walker on November 26, 1832. Mary, her four older sisters, and a younger brother lived with their parents on a farm near Oswego, New York. Alvah Walker worked as a carpenter and was an avid reader with an interest in medicine. He believed strongly in social reform, particularly where his daughters were concerned. Unlike many men of the period, he felt that girls should be educated and encouraged to pursue professional careers. Two of Mary's older sisters attended a local school and later furthered their education at Falley Seminary, an academy for girls in Fulton, New York.

Mary's father also had strong views about women's clothing, especially the tight corsets that contorted women's bodies to achieve the fashionably tiny waistlines of the period. He thought they caused medical problems, so he would not allow his daughters to wear the tight undergarments.

Alvah Walker believed most women's fashions were unhealthy. Breathing was hampered by corsets that dangerously constricted the wearer's midsection, while the long flowing skirts dragged on the ground, picking up dirt. His daughter Mary took his views to heart.

When Alvah Walker was ill for two winters in a row, he turned to his medical books for cures to his ailments. Thumbing through his books piqued young Mary's curiosity and an idea took root. Already planning a professional career, she quickly developed an interest in the study of medicine.

Unfortunately, the Walkers didn't have enough money for Mary to receive a medical education. So, in 1852, she took a teaching position in the village of Minetto, New York, and began to save money for medical school. Mary knew that becoming a doctor would be an uphill battle because almost no medical schools were admitting women at that time. Several years earlier, Geneva College of Medicine had accepted Elizabeth Blackwell, but other schools were slow to open their doors to female students.

While teaching and saving money, Mary applied to a number of medical schools. Like Blackwell, she received a string of rejections, but her persistence eventually paid off with acceptance into New York's Syracuse Medical College. In December 1853, at the age of 21, she began working toward her medical degree.

Mary studied a broad curriculum at Syracuse. After the introductory anatomy classes, she learned the basics of performing surgery. She studied childbirth in obstetrics classes and was taught the composition of drugs and how to administer them in chemistry and pharmacy classes. But her most important lesson—and the one she took with her into the Civil War less than 10 years later—was one Syracuse stressed above all others: a doctor should never prescribe a remedy that could cause more harm than the original ailment.

Although this tenet seems obvious today, in the 1850s many "cures" made their patients more sick than their illnesses had. For example, *bloodletting*—cutting to induce bleeding—as a treatment for illness still enjoyed popularity at the time. But that procedure often left the patient weak from loss of blood and sometimes even caused death. Amputation of an injured limb was another suspect treatment. Walker believed that everything possible should be done to save a damaged arm or leg, and she later rejected the shortsighted reliance on amputation during the Civil War.

The soldiers recuperating at this Civil War aid station provide vivid examples of the widespread use of amputation as a treatment for battlefield wounds.

When Mary and her classmates finally marched forward to receive their medical degrees in June 1855, she was the only woman in the group. Like Elizabeth Blackwell seven years before, Mary Walker had broken into the male-dominated field of medicine.

Five months after graduation, Walker married Dr. Albert Miller. During a marriage that would last only four years, the couple settled in Rome, New York, and set up a medical practice together. Already considered unconventional for studying medicine, Walker further offended Rome's citizens when she declined to take her husband's last name or to swear obedience in her marriage vows. Although not uncommon today, in the 1850s such actions went completely against tradition.

Unhappy in their marriage, Walker and Miller separated in 1859 and finally divorced many years later. After this disappointment, Dr. Walker moved from the home she had shared with her husband and continued to practice medicine on her own. When the Civil War erupted in 1861, she traveled to Washington, D.C., hoping to lend her medical skills to the federal government's war effort. Immediately upon her arrival in the nation's capital, she applied for a commission in the Union Army. A commission would give her the military rank of an officer and authorize her to receive a salary for her efforts.

The impatient Dr. Walker didn't bother to wait for the army's response, however. Instead, she plunged into volunteer service. By the time the military informed her that it had refused her application for a commission, she was already working for Dr. J. N. Green, the surgeon in charge of a makeshift hospital that had been set up in the Patent Office in Washington. Despite the army's rejection, Walker kept reapplying. Eventually, she went directly to the Surgeon General of the United States—the chief medical officer of the army. Then she wrote to President Abraham Lincoln. Still Dr. Walker received no commission for her work.

Dedicated to her patients, Walker continued to work without pay, sleeping in an alcove at the hospital and eating hospital rations. She discovered that her volunteer status offered her at least one advantage that she wouldn't have as an officer: she was free to drop lesser duties when something more important arose. As a result, Walker could take time to escort wounded soldiers to their homes so their families could care for them. No job was too large or too small for Walker, and she worked long hours, acting as physician, hospital administrator, counselor—and even religious confessor—for the 100 or so homesick soldiers housed in the hospital.

As the war raged on, Dr. Walker found her own way to the battlefields. In autumn 1862, she arrived at the village of Warrenton, Virginia, where a field hospital had been hastily constructed. The emergency conditions were terrible. She found a severe shortage of supplies and only a few overworked and exhausted medical personnel. Tirelessly, Walker pitched in, helping wherever she could.

Walker worked at a Warrenton, Virginia, field hospital similar to this one. Trying to meet a shortage of medical supplies, Walker recalled that to make bandages "I went to my trunk, took out four pretty nightgowns, [and] tore them into small squares."

Bleeding soldiers from the nearby battlegrounds filled the hospital to capacity. She and the other doctors had time enough only to rush from patient to patient, stepping over the cold bodies of the dead to offer meager emergency care to those who were still breathing.

The injuries were worse than anything Walker had ever seen. One soldier had a head wound so terrible that she could see his brain pulsing through a gaping hole in his skull. And with very little medicine and almost no bandages, the troops suffered horribly from painful infections. When she realized that some of the wounded could receive far better care in Washington, Walker pressured the army's leadership until General Ambrose Burnside allowed her to organize and oversee the transportation of the injured to the capital, about 40 miles away.

Not all of Walker's contributions were so visible, however. Many were simple acts of thoughtfulness. For instance, she once observed soldiers carrying patients downhill with their heads lower than their feet. Realizing how uncomfortable this must be for the patients, she stopped the soldiers and admonished them to carry a wounded patient feet first down a hill.

Another time, Dr. Walker launched a search for the mother of a drummer boy who had lost both feet in battle and was being transported to the army hospital in Washington. The young boy was dying, and Dr. Walker refused to end her search until she had located the boy's mother to break the news. The woman was a widow with no other means of support than her dying son. Ever resourceful, Walker found the distraught mother a job helping to care for the injured.

After months of toiling on the battlefields, the exhausted Walker returned to the capital in 1863. As she strolled around the city, she noticed hundreds of women apparently living on the streets. They had come to the city to visit their wounded husbands and sons but could find no place to stay. Walker again reacted immediately. She approached local women's groups and appealed to wealthy women to provide relief for their destitute sisters. With their contributions, Walker organized the Women's Relief Association, which offered aid not only to women visiting wounded soldiers, but also to other impoverished women in the city. Dr. Walker even implemented a counseling system to determine the causes of the women's poverty so they could receive more specific help.

Walker had always been assertive and keenly observant. Whenever she saw a problem, she always tried to fix it, and her actions in the current crisis were no exception. Late in 1863, she visited the Union Army's Deserters' Prison in Alexandria, Virginia. When she spoke to the inmates, she realized that some of the men were unjustly imprisoned. For instance, one boy had left his regiment only to visit his dying mother. Without delay, she went directly to the War Office. The boy was pardoned, and Walker secured a pass and an escort for the young soldier so he could go to his mother's deathbed.

On the battlefields and in the hospitals, Walker witnessed dreadful conditions and suffering soldiers. Many of the injuries she saw were to the men's arms and legs. Because a wound could quickly become infected under battlefield conditions, surgeons usually just amputated the injured limb. It was quicker than trying to heal the wounded arms and legs—and it was better in the days before antibiotics to sacrifice the limb than to risk a soldier's death from infection.

Although the surgeons may have believed they were doing the best thing, Dr. Walker disagreed. Battlefield amputations could be fatal because of the unsanitary conditions of the field hospitals. Thus, the practice violated Syracuse Medical College's warning not to choose remedies that were worse than the original ailment. Walker was convinced that the surgeons were much too eager to remove limbs, and she believed that some attempt should always be made to heal the wounded arm or leg.

Walker decided to change the situation. Knowing she might be forced to leave if she consulted her superiors, she chose another route. Walker went directly to the patients and talked them into resisting amputation. She even encouraged patients to threaten bodily harm to the surgeons if they persisted. Her crusade no doubt fueled the growing controversy over the use of amputation that raged until the end of the war.

In late September 1863, Dr. Walker headed to Chattanooga, Tennessee, to help in the aftermath of the bloody battle of Chickamauga. Her valuable service caught the attention of the army's high command, and she was assigned to be an assistant surgeon in the 52nd Ohio Regiment in January 1864. Walker had finally achieved official status with the Union Army.

Walker experienced grisly sights even worse than this in the aftermath of Chickamauga, the bloodiest two-day battle of the Civil War.

As the regiment enjoyed the relative quiet of winter quarters, Dr. Walker ventured out to aid civilians in the area. She even crossed into Confederate territory several times to reach patients after the other army physicians had refused for fear of being captured. Taking pity on the impoverished residents of the area, she treated people suffering from typhoid fever, helped to deliver babies, and even extracted teeth.

As the other doctors had feared, while on a mission behind Confederate lines on April 10, 1864, Walker fell into the hands of enemy troops. She was placed under arrest and shipped off to Castle Thunder, a rebel prison in Richmond, Virginia. A converted tobacco warehouse, Castle Thunder was unbearably hot and humid during the four months Walker was imprisoned. While she was behind bars, she had to sleep on a filthy mattress infested with insects. At night she often lay awake stifled by the foul air and listening to the patter of rodents scurrying over the dirty floors. Finally she was released in a prisoner exchange in August.

After her capture by Confederate troops, Walker spent four months in Castle Thunder, a Confederate prison.

Upon her release from prison, the army ordered Dr. Walker to go to Louisville, Kentucky, as an assistant surgeon in charge of the female patients in that city's prison hospital. Because these women were mostly Confederates accused of spying, Dr. Walker faced immediate hostility. To make matters worse, the doctor who had been in charge of the entire facility resented his demotion to running only the men's hospital, so he offered Walker little support. Dr. Walker's new patients were also put off by her no-nonsense style, a product of her time on the front lines. After several months in this thankless job, she requested a transfer back to the battlefront. Instead, the army assigned her to an orphanage in Clarkesville, Tennessee, where she spent the last months of the war in relative peace and quiet.

After the war, Walker's work with the destitute citizens around Chattanooga was officially acknowledged when President Andrew Johnson presented her with the Congressional Medal of Honor, the nation's highest award for valor. Walker, noted the president, had "devoted herself with patriotic zeal to the sick and wounded," even "to the detriment of her own health." It was a proud moment for Walker, and she wore the medal for the rest of her life.

With her wartime duties behind her, Walker remained in Washington, D.C., to practice medicine. Soon, however, she found her interest drawn to social issues affecting women. She gave up being a physician when she took on a new challenge and became involved in the women's suffrage movement to gain voting rights for women. Walker wisely used her unique position as the only female doctor to have served in the Union Army to publicize the cause of suffrage activists. Working with the Central Women's Suffrage Bureau of Washington, she lectured, attended congressional hearings, and even attempted to cast her vote in an election in her hometown of Oswego.

While some western states enfranchised women in the nineteenth century—Wyoming, for example, gave women the right to vote in 1869—most states prohibited their female citizens from voting until forced to do so by the Nineteenth Amendment in 1920.

Walker also continued her work in the area of dress reform and was elected president of the National Dress Reform Association in 1866. Like her father, Walker considered fashions for women not only cumbersome and unsanitary, but also physically dangerous. The many yards of fabric that went into the lengthy skirts of the day swept the floor like a broom, collecting grime. And because small waists were fashionable, women often laced their corsets so tight they displaced their internal organs.

During the war, Walker would have nothing to do with dresses. Instead, she clad herself in a Union officer's blue uniform: pants with gold stripes, a felt hat encircled by a gold cord, and a bright green surgeon's sash about her waist. Walker continued to reject traditional female clothing after the war and eventually took to wearing a full men's suit—including a bow tie and top hat!—to publicize her defiant stance on dress reform.

Following her father's death in 1880, Walker retired to the family farm in New York to care for her aging mother. She never returned to medicine but instead spent her remaining years speaking and writing about the women's issues that most concerned her. Only after a fall on the steps of the Capitol building in Washington, D.C., did she slow her energetic pace. Never recovering from her accident, she died in Oswego on February 21, 1919, at the age of 86.

In Mary Edwards Walker, soldiers and civilians alike found someone who genuinely cared about their health.

Walker remained true to her beliefs to the end of her life, including her preference for pants over dresses. The Congressional Medal of Honor was her most cherished possession, and she never went anywhere without the award pinned to her jacket.

While many people today might not remember her name, they have benefited from her life's efforts. Numerous female physicians in the military follow Walker's selfless example of serving sick and wounded soldiers both in peacetime and on the battlefield.

Susan La Flesche Picotte (1865-1915) as a medical student in the late 1880s. Soon after she sat for this portrait, La Flesche Picotte became the first female American Indian doctor in the United States.

3

Susan La Flesche Picotte
A Bridge for Her People

*I*n autumn 1915, a group of mourners stood solemnly in Dr. Susan La Flesche Picotte's living room. The sad gathering had come to say farewell to their beloved friend who had spent her life serving the people of the Omaha American Indian tribe. Three men had come to conduct the funeral. Two were from the reservation's small Presbyterian church, where La Flesche Picotte had worshiped. They spoke first. Then they stood aside as the third, an aged Omaha man, offered up a prayer in his native language.

That Susan's funeral was conducted in both English and Omaha was fitting, for her life had straddled two colliding worlds. By the 1860s, the Omaha Indians could no longer live as they had for uncounted generations. The buffalo, the Omahas' traditional source of food and clothing, were being wiped out by the oncoming rush of whites. Fifty million buffalo grazed North America's grasslands in 1850. Only about 50 of them would remain 33 years later. To escape a similar fate, the Omaha would need to adapt to their changing environment. Susan La Flesche Picotte, the first American Indian woman to

Wholesale slaughter of the buffalo by whites destroyed the traditional way of life for many American Indian groups of the Great Plains region.

become a doctor, spent her life helping her people adjust to a different way of living.

La Flesche Picotte was continuing the work of her father, Chief Joseph La Flesche. Known to his people as Iron Eye, Chief Joseph, who was part French, had been one of the first Omaha Indians to build a "white man's" log house. He sent his own children to school off the reservation because he felt this experience would better prepare them for living in American culture. Since whites had overrun lands formerly promised to the Plains Indians, Chief Joseph could see no other alternative.

Chief Joseph's previous contacts with Europeans had convinced him that the Omaha's traditional way of life could never survive the steady encroachment of white settlers—and especially their alcohol. The Omaha, he reasoned, must learn the ways of the whites without succumbing to their vices.

Susan was born into the changing world of the Omaha on June 17, 1865. She was the fifth and youngest child of Chief Joseph and his wife, Mary, known as The One Woman. Like Susan, many members of the La Flesche family in adulthood would dedicate themselves to serving the community. One sister, Susette, would later lecture around the country to raise awareness of the poor treatment of American Indians. Another sister, Rosalie, would keep the records for the various funds established by people wanting to help the Omaha as a result of Susette's talks. Marguerite, a third sister, would become a teacher at the reservation school. Their selfless attitudes greatly influenced young Susan.

When Susan was 14, Chief Joseph sent her and Marguerite to New Jersey to go to school at the Elizabeth Institute for Young Ladies, where Susette had studied earlier. In New Jersey, Susan's English improved daily, and she gained valuable experience interacting with others whose backgrounds differed completely from hers.

After returning home to Nebraska in 1882, Susan steadily grew more concerned about her people's welfare. Her eyes opened to the problems among the families on the reservation. Children and adults went hungry and were often sick, and their homes were in constant disrepair. Longing to help, Susan took a teaching position at the reservation's mission school.

The root of the problem faced by the Omaha in 1882 was the federal government's erratic—and often brutal—policy toward all American Indians. In 1830, Congress had passed the Indian Removal Act, which called for the forced resettlement of American Indians to lands west of the Mississippi River. By the mid-1850s, as white settlers pushed beyond the great river in increasing numbers, the native groups were further confined to reservations. Faced with the whites' insatiable appetite for land and the U.S. government's refusal to keep its treaty promises, Chief Joseph La Flesche and other Omaha leaders had been forced to sign away much of their traditional hunting grounds in 1854.

The loss of their hunting lands and the destruction of the buffalo led to drastic changes for the Omaha. In the late 1850s, Chief Joseph replaced his earth lodge with a log-framed house. As the Omaha moved to the reservation, their traditional ways of life went the way of the earth lodge. Susan's people were bitter, depressed, and unsure how to live in the white man's world.

Around the time Susan returned from New Jersey, she helped the white reservation doctor take care of Alice Fletcher, an anthropologist friend of her father's who had suffered a badly broken leg. Nursing Fletcher made Susan question the quality of medical care on the reservation. The doctor didn't seem to care about his patients, most of whom preferred to suffer than go to him. Many people still trusted their health to Omaha medicine men and women, who healed with traditional herbal remedies, sweat baths, and songs and prayers. Susan believed the Omahas needed good modern medical care. And then it occurred to her: Perhaps *she* could study medicine and become the physician for her people.

From the beginning, Susan understood that becoming a doctor was difficult even for white women and that no American Indian woman had ever earned a medical degree. But the more Susan thought about her new idea, the more sense it made to her. Determination, she believed, would get her over the obstacles. When she and Marguerite again left home in 1884 to attend the Hampton Normal and Agricultural Institute in Virginia,

Susan had almost made up her mind to pursue the study of medicine.

As she had been at the Elizabeth Institute five years earlier, Susan was again exposed to a host of new experiences and people. For one thing, the school was coeducational, with young men and women studying together. This policy differed greatly from Omaha tradition, which stressed that young men and women should never be left alone together. Susan adjusted well and even fell in love for the first time, but her relationship was short-lived. Becoming a doctor, she decided, was more important than romance.

At Hampton Susan met Dr. Martha M. Waldron, who served as the institute's doctor. Waldron's example as one of the nation's few female doctors cemented Susan's conviction to study medicine. She doubled her efforts and excelled in all areas at Hampton.

Susan's hard work paid off. Besides being presented with a gold medal for outstanding scholastic achievement, Hampton's officials selected her to address her class members during her graduation ceremony in 1886.

By the time Susan graduated from Hampton, she had already gained acceptance into the Woman's Medical College of Pennsylvania, the same Philadelphia school that Dr. Waldron had attended. The cost of medical school had posed a real problem, but now even that worry was gone. The Women's National Indian Association, a group devoted to providing professional training for

The Female (later Woman's) Medical College of Pennsylvania was founded in 1850 by William Mullen. That year, the first eight female students were taught by a faculty made up entirely of men.

American Indians, had awarded Susan a grant to pay for her education.

The study of medicine at the Woman's Medical College came naturally to Susan, and she again performed well. The work was hard, but the classes fascinated her.

When she wasn't studying, Susan found time to explore Philadelphia and visit the homes of the many white friends she made at school. Her friendships were living reminders of her father's belief that the Omaha must learn to get along with whites.

In the spring of 1889, at the age of 23, Susan completed the three-year course in just two years, graduating at the top of her class of 36. But graduation day brought mixed emotions for her because she was unable to share with her father her pride at being the first American Indian woman to graduate from medical school. Chief Joseph had died just a few months earlier. "You don't know how it felt to receive my degree and not to have him there," a somber Susan wrote to a former teacher.

During the remainder of 1889, Susan completed an internship at the Woman's Hospital in Philadelphia. Then Dr. La Flesche headed back to the reservation to serve as the children's physician at the government school. Now she could assist her people by being their doctor and also by helping to bridge the gap between the Omaha and white cultures.

The new doctor's first order of business was to examine every one of her young patients. La Flesche felt the Omaha children had lived too long without adequate medical care. During her examinations, she took great pains to make the children feel safe and welcome, a consideration she later would extend to their distrustful parents. Dr. La Flesche instructed the school's teachers to send their students to her two at a time so no one would have to be alone during the exam.

Susan worked daily with the children on the reservation. Before long, she realized that many of their problems, such as infected cuts, could be prevented if their parents learned how to treat minor wounds. Her opportunity to work with the parents came when the U.S.

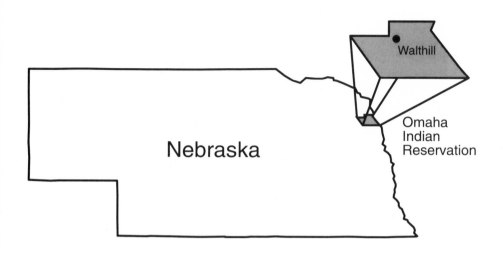

Before the Omaha moved to their Thurston County, Nebraska, reservation in 1854, they owned more than 20 times as much land, covering more than one-third of what is now the state of Nebraska.

government appointed La Flesche as the physician for the reservation's adults as well as the children.

Proud of her new position, Susan decided she would be the best physician her people ever had. Unfortunately, her 1,300 patients lived widely scattered across the reservation, which stretched more than 26 miles east and west and was about 14 miles from its southernmost points to its northern boundaries. So Dr. La Flesche was forced to ride long distances on horseback to see her patients.

She never refused a call. More than once she and her faithful horse, Pie, braved blinding snowstorms to reach a patient. Susan broke dozens of medicine bottles and thermometers bouncing over the rough terrain until she finally bought a carriage. Even then, the demands of her practice remained grueling.

During her first four years as the tribe's physician, La Flesche taught her patients how improved hygiene and sanitation could prevent infections, parasites, and the spread of disease. She encouraged the Omaha people to cover their food to protect it from flies and to avoid using the same water cup with a family member who was ill. Dr. La Flesche cautioned her patients to clean their cooking areas and to wash their hands before handling food, and she also taught them how to treat minor injuries. Seeing their doctor's commitment to their welfare caused the Omahas' trust in Susan and her modern medical care to grow.

After four years at this relentless pace, La Flesche began to experience headaches. Soon she was feeling a pain in her ears as well. At first, she worked through the nagging aches. But as they intensified, La Flesche was unable to maintain the level of care she had given her patients in the past. Only reluctantly did she finally surrender her proud position as the government physician for the Omaha.

Soon after her resignation, Susan married Henry Picotte, the brother of her sister Marguerite's husband, in 1894. Dr. La Flesche Picotte, as she was now called, settled into married life in the reservation town of Bancroft, Nebraska, and quickly bore two sons. Although she could

La Flesche Picotte sits on the front porch of her house in Bancroft, Nebraska, with her two sons and her mother, The One Woman.

no longer keep her arduous schedule of traveling across the reservation, Susan still hoped to continue a medical practice, which she operated out of her home. She encouraged patients to visit her at any hour, and she even left a lamp burning in her front window to light the way to her doorstep.

Chief Joseph had striven to rid the reservation of alcohol, and Susan shared his commitment. Her conviction only deepened when her husband died of alcoholism in 1905. The following year, when the town of Walthill was founded on the reservation, La Flesche Picotte traveled to Washington, D.C., to meet with the Secretary of the Interior. Responding to Susan's insistence, the U.S. Congress passed a law forbidding the sale of liquor in the new town.

La Flesche Picotte moved to Walthill later that year. In spite of her continuing headaches and earaches, she threw herself into the community, eager to transform it into a haven for sober and healthy living. She helped organize the county medical society and became active in the affairs of the local Presbyterian church. La Flesche Picotte also soon took over as health officer for Walthill. A member of the state medical society, she lobbied Nebraska's state legislature for better laws regarding public health.

Although her accomplishments grew steadily, one goal still eluded Dr. La Flesche Picotte. Since her days at the Hampton Institute, she had hoped to build a hospital on the Omaha Reservation in order to avoid having to send her patients to Sioux City, Iowa. About 20 miles from the reservation's border, Sioux City was a long distance at a time when automobiles were rare. Previous attempts to establish a hospital had failed due to a lack of money, but Susan's dream eventually came true in 1913.

To bring medical care closer to the seriously ill and injured, La Flesche Picotte had this hospital built in the town of Walthill, Nebraska, in 1913.

With the reservation's support, she was able to raise enough money. The Omaha would finally have a hospital.

At La Flesche Picotte's direction, the hospital was constructed in Walthill on a prominent hill overlooking the reservation. A firm believer in the healing quality of fresh air, she insisted that the building be dotted with windows and have a spacious, covered porch where patients could relax and enjoy the outdoors.

Besides providing medical care, Dr. La Flesche Picotte did everything she could to familiarize her people with white culture, including Christianity. As the first

American Indian appointed to be a missionary by the Presbyterian Board of Home Missions, Susan spread her faith by teaching Sunday-school classes and reading aloud passages from the Bible in the Omaha language. Not all her efforts succeeded, however, and one in particular was even amusing. Once she talked a young Omaha couple into having a Presbyterian church wedding instead of the traditional Omaha ceremony. When the minister declared the couple married, they froze, not knowing what to do next. Finally, the bride and groom simply turned around and left the church—walking down separate aisles!

Even though she taught white culture and religion to the Omaha, La Flesche Picotte never lost her love for her native heritage. She sometimes wore traditional Omaha clothes for special events, such as the graduation ceremonies of her younger patients. In addition, Susan wrote numerous articles about tribal customs and American Indian legends for reservation newspapers. By adopting modern medical practices and Christianity while still maintaining a reverence for Omaha traditions, La Flesche Picotte helped to bridge the divide between the two cultures.

Susan's years of hard work took a great toll on her health. Along with her headaches and earaches, she suffered from a painful infection of her facial bones. In 1915, she underwent two operations in an attempt to correct the problem, but both were unsuccessful. On

September 15, 1915, Susan La Flesche Picotte died. She was only 50 years old.

Susan's commitment to the Omaha never wavered. Legend says that in her 25 years of work as a physician, she treated every single member of the Omaha tribe. But La Flesche Picotte was more than a successful doctor. She helped many of the Omaha to find a way to adjust to cultural changes without losing their heritage. Characteristically, La Flesche Picotte had once told a government official that she would "willingly and gladly cooperate in anything that is for the good of the tribe." But, also in character, she warned that she would "fight good and hard against anything that is to the tribe's detriment, even if I have to fight alone." Only death forced her to give up that fight.

*To recognize May Edward Chinn's distinguished
medical career and service to the public, Columbia
University awarded her an honorary degree.*

4

May Edward Chinn
The Accidental Doctor

*M*ay Chinn had no idea that her freshmen research paper about sewage disposal would change the course of her life. She was a music major and had only signed up for the hygiene class to fill a space in her schedule. To May's astonishment, Dr. Jean Broadhurst, the professor who had assigned the paper, was so impressed by her report that she told May the right field for her was science, not music. "So the second year I changed my Major to Science under Dr. Broadhurst," remembered Chinn, and "the remaining three years were wonderful."

"I never expected such an interesting paper from a person whose major is music," Professor Jean Broadhurst told Chinn after reading her work. This conversation would change the young student's life.

Despite the fact that May's future career came to her almost by accident, she was remarkably well suited for a future in science and medicine that would see her emerge as one of America's pioneering black female doctors. Her natural curiosity fueled her passionate interest in cancer research. And the selflessness learned from her mother—who, May remembered in later years, "scrubbed floors" so her daughter could further her education—inspired May to provide care for her patients even when they could not afford to pay her.

May Edward Chinn was born in Great Barrington, Massachusetts, on April 15, 1896. Her father, William Lafayette Chinn, had been born a slave in Virginia and was 13 when the Civil War ended in 1865. Having grown up without an education, William later opposed any college instruction for his daughter as a ridiculous idea. In stark contrast, May's mother, Lula Ann, dreamed of her daughter having a university degree, and she worked long hours at two jobs to save money for May's education.

In 1918, Chinn took a barrage of tests at New York City's Teachers College (part of Columbia University). Even though she had not finished high school, her scores were high enough to allow her to enter the college's music program. Towards the end of her first year at school, she found herself one credit short of her goal for the year. To obtain the credit, she took a course in hygiene. It was in that class that May wrote the sewage paper that would lead to her career in medicine.

May Chinn never regretted her decision to change her major from music to science. Although she continued her voice lessons and enjoyed the occasional gatherings with friends to play music and sing, she knew that her future lay in medicine.

May's hygiene professor, Dr. Broadhurst, became almost a second mother to the young woman. She advised May and employed her as her assistant. In addition, Broadhurst arranged for May to gain hands-on experience in the field of *clinical pathology*, the study of the

The main hall of Teachers College in 1920

origin and nature of disease in a clinical setting, by working directly with patients. This work helped May land a
job in clinical pathology even before she graduated from
Teachers College in 1921.

Ironically, it was May's background in music that
helped her get into medical school. In late 1921, the
assistant dean of Bellevue Hospital Medical College in
New York City interviewed her for admission. May
arrived prepared to discuss her future in medicine, but
when the dean learned she had played the piano with the
famous black singer Paul Robeson for several years, he

became so excited that he spent most of the interview talking about Robeson. When he finally got around to asking May why she wanted to study medicine, she had only five short minutes to reply!

The letter of acceptance to medical school delighted May, and she eagerly entered the Bellevue Hospital Medical College (now the New York University Medical College) in 1922. For four years, she endured the strenuous pace of medical school until that groundbreaking day in 1926 when she became the first black woman in Bellevue's history to receive a medical diploma.

Bellevue Hospital Medical College, where Chinn began her medical studies in 1922, was founded in 1860.

Dr. May Chinn toppled another barrier later that year when she interned at New York City's predominantly white Harlem Hospital—the first African American woman to do so. She soon discovered, however, that other doors remained shut to her. While white doctors could freely work in New York City's hospitals and clinics, black physicians could find no hospitals to hire them. Working in a hospital would have provided not only a place for May's patients who needed surgery, but it also would have given her the opportunity to observe a number of different diseases firsthand and to study the effects of new drugs being developed.

Unable to find a position at a hospital, Dr. Chinn decided to treat patients privately in Harlem, a mostly black area of the city that was thriving in the 1920s. But May still needed the help of Harlem's established black male doctors in order to get started. At first, many of the doctors ignored her. Others offered what they considered help by letting Chinn handle some of their house calls. Unfortunately for the new doctor, they usually gave her the cases that needed to be seen after midnight!

Gradually, however, Chinn earned the other doctors' respect. Some, in fact, even began asking her to treat members of their own families. "It was then," Chinn later recalled, that "I felt I was finally accepted as a physician practicing in their neighborhood as one of them."

Denied hospital access, Chinn and other black doctors invented new ways of performing surgery on their

Although African Americans had been moving to Harlem in great numbers since 1910, in the mid-1920s, the vast majority of the staff of Harlem Hospital was still white.

patients. Chinn could handle the minor cases in her office, but major surgery was another matter. She and the attending surgeon often operated in a patient's own home, where the conditions were usually crude. To sterilize her gowns and surgical dressings, for instance, Chinn baked them in the kitchen oven. Then, while her clothes were baking, she sterilized her surgical utensils by boiling them on the stove. Finally, when everything was ready, the doctor operated, sometimes with the patient lying on an ironing board! While the circumstances were less than satisfactory, Chinn remembered having "the best 'nurses' in the world"—the patients' own family members.

Many of Chinn's patients were aged and had little extra money for medicine. Unable to bear their suffering, she often gave them medication at no charge. Chinn's generosity helped in another way as well. Hospitals terrified many of her older patients, who thought people only went to the hospital to die. Chinn understood this and instead brought the hospital to them.

It was while making house calls during her second year of practice that May acquired an interest in cancer research. As she later explained, "I suspected that many of the patients who I saw in their homes were what we now call 'terminal cancer' patients." They were simply wasting away from what Dr. Chinn suspected was the advanced stages of cancer. She was determined to find some way of detecting the disease earlier so she could treat it.

In her quest to understand cancer, Chinn visited hospitals that dealt with the deadly disease, hoping to learn from the male doctors who worked with cancer patients. When they refused to help her, Chinn had an idea. If she could accompany one of her patients to a cancer hospital, perhaps the physician on duty would allow her to observe her patient's examination.

Chinn's idea worked. She not only learned how to check a patient for signs of cancer and how to take a *biopsy*—a procedure in which a doctor takes a sample from a suspicious lump in order to test it for cancer—but she also discovered where hospitals sent the biopsies for diagnosis. Back in her office, Dr. Chinn began taking biopsies herself and sending them to the same place for testing. She could then diagnose cancer at a much earlier stage in its development, which greatly increased the odds for successful treatment.

Chinn's appetite for cancer research was now whetted. In 1928, she began studying with Dr. George Papanicolaou, whose research focused on early cancer detection in women. Having discovered that the wall of the uterus continuously sheds cells, Papanicolaou believed it possible to test these cells for cancer. Dr. Chinn was part of his research team that explored different ways of testing cells in order to find the cancerous ones as early as possible. (Today, Papanicolaou is best known for his development in 1943 of the Pap smear examination, a procedure that makes possible the early detection of cervical cancer in women.) May was thrilled to study with such a brilliant physician, and she remained on his team for the next five years. Two decades later, from 1948 to 1955, Chinn would again work with Dr. Papanicolaou.

But Dr. Chinn refused to limit her career to cancer research. To serve as many people as possible, she often held several different positions simultaneously. Beginning in 1928, Chinn served for 50 years as a physician for a Catholic convent of African American nuns called the Franciscan Handmaids of Mary. In 1945, Dr. Elsie S. L'Esperance, a physician known for her extensive work in

George Papanicolaou (1883-1962), with whom Chinn began studying in 1928, pioneered the Pap smear, a technique still widely used to test for cervical cancer.

cancer research, invited Chinn to join the staff of the Strang Clinic, part of the New York Infirmary for Women and Children. She stayed with the Strang Clinic as a cancer specialist for the next 29 years. Then, in 1961, Chinn traveled to France and Italy as the physician for a group of severely disabled people.

Dr. Chinn constantly sought innovative methods of treating her patients. Because the practice of medicine was continuously evolving, she needed to keep abreast of the most up-to-date medical procedures and research findings. In 1933, she went back to school and earned a master of science degree in public health from Columbia University, the same institution from which she had received her undergraduate degree. Chinn also furthered her education at medical seminars in Europe, Japan, and throughout North America.

Children always held a special place in Dr. Chinn's heart. Throughout her busy career, she always maintained at least one clinic devoted solely to the treatment of children. (At one point, she operated three.) Besides her own facilities, Chinn spent the 17 years between 1960 and 1977 as the clinician for the Department of Health day-care centers operating in New York City.

Chinn's years of service earned her many awards. In 1957, the New York City Cancer Committee of the American Cancer Society presented her an honorary citation for her work on Papanicolaou's research team. Another citation, awarded to her in 1977 for 50 years of devoted service to the black community, came from the Susan Smith McKinney Steward, M.D., Society. New York City's Columbia University, Chinn's alma mater, awarded her an honorary doctorate two years later. Following Columbia's lead, New York University bestowed an honorary doctor of science degree upon *its* former student in June 1980.

Not even her 1977 retirement slowed down May Chinn. She had always counseled young people to "become involved with the problems of your nation, your

Columbia University figured prominently in Chinn's life, awarding her three different degrees—a bachelor's degree in 1921, a master's degree 12 years later, and then an honorary doctorate in 1979.

state, your city," and she followed her own advice by remaining active in various health-related and professional organizations. At the national level, May worked with an educational foundation, the Phelps-Stokes Fund, to bring medical students from Africa and other parts of the world to the United States to study. She also retained her memberships in the American Cancer Society and the National Council of Women of the United States.

In addition, Chinn served on several medical committees in the New York City area.

Although she lived a long and rich life, May Chinn's years as a physician brought her little wealth. In fact, because she refused to charge her patients who couldn't afford her services, she lived frugally during the last years of her life. Her main sustenance proved not to be money, but a religious faith that emphasized "brotherhood and the practice of brotherhood." On December 1, 1980, Dr. Chinn attended a reception honoring not her own lifetime of accomplishment, but that of a friend. While at the reception, she collapsed and died from a heart attack at the age of 84.

Thanks to a mother's dream, an unusually good research paper, and a professor who took an interest in an exceptionally bright pupil, the people of Harlem benefited from the devotion and care of Dr. May Edward Chinn for over 50 years. Her desire to heal other people's pain was matched only by her drive to overcome the difficulties she had faced in the early years of her practice when, for a time, she was Harlem's only African American female physician. "Help those with problems," Chinn said simply. "Help them to take the next step—UPWARDS."

Working with infants her entire career, Helen Brooke Taussig (1898-1986) pioneered a cure for the heart problems of "blue babies."

5

Helen Brooke Taussig
Queen of Hearts

*H*unched over the family dining table, Helen frowned at her book. She had been there for hours, slowly reading one word at a time, but the words seemed to change as she stared at them. Even though she thought she saw the word *was*, she just wasn't sure. Maybe it was *saw*.

She tried to understand the word in the context of the other words around it, but that didn't work either. Frustrated, Helen slammed the book shut. She loved to learn, but how could she if she couldn't read? As usual, it was her father who reassured her with his sense of humor.

"Helen," he chuckled, "spelling is not logical. You are a very logical girl; no wonder you can't spell!" Encouraged by his support, she worked on reading for hours every day.

Today, specialists know that Helen suffered from *dyslexia*, a reading disorder that causes letters and words to appear distorted or reversed on the page. But Helen never let herself fall into despair even though the condition often left her embarrassed in school. To her, dyslexia was just another challenge she expected to master. By dealing with dyslexia, Helen developed an extraordinary ability to solve problems. Eventually, she utilized her skill to devise an operation that saved the lives of thousands of "blue babies."

Life began for Helen Brooke Taussig on May 24, 1898, in Cambridge, Massachusetts, where she was born into a family of scholars. Helen's mother, Edith Guild Taussig, had studied biology and botany at Radcliffe College. Her father, Professor Frank William Taussig, spent 53 years at Harvard as a distinguished economist.

The Taussig family enjoyed summers at their comfortable Cape Cod home. Adhering to their parents' philosophy of never wasting a minute of the day, Helen and her sisters and brother studied in the mornings and played and relaxed in the evenings. The children loved the outdoors—swimming in the blue ocean and hiking along the shore.

Unfortunately, Helen's idyllic childhood ended suddenly when she was 9 years old. Her mother contracted

Frank William Taussig was an eminent Harvard professor who loved teaching.

tuberculosis, a dreaded disease of the lungs that claimed many lives in the early 1900s. Despite the loving care Edith Taussig received, she never recovered from this disease. By the time Helen was 11, her mother was dead.

Following her mother's death, Helen drew closer to her father. Throughout her teenage years, she continued to struggle with dyslexia. But with her father's help and encouragement, she managed to improve her reading well enough to graduate from high school and attend college. As Helen later wrote, she was beginning to learn "the importance of carrying through to completion any project I undertook."

Helen enrolled in Cambridge's highly regarded Radcliffe College in March 1917. An avid athlete, she enthusiastically participated on the school's tennis and basketball teams. But she wasn't comfortable at Radcliffe because her father's well-known academic reputation left her feeling overshadowed. After two years, believing that "it would be a good idea for me to get away and stand on my own feet," Helen transferred across the country to the prestigious University of California at Berkeley.

Helen enjoyed her independence at Berkeley. The adventurous young woman would go on hikes to remote sections of California's Yosemite National Park, a challenging expedition in the early twentieth century when the park was much less developed than it is today.

Following her graduation from Berkeley in 1921, Taussig faced the decision of what career choice to make. Interested in medicine, she took a course at Harvard Medical School that focused on the tissues of the human body. Harvard let Taussig enroll in the class, but, she recalled, she had to sit apart from the men so she would not "contaminate" them. In addition, the school had a policy against allowing women into the medical-degree program.

Dr. John Lewis Bremer, Taussig's professor at Harvard, realized that his bright young student was wasting her abilities. No matter how well she did in his class, Harvard wouldn't let her study anatomy and would never grant her a medical degree. (It was not until 1945 that

Harvard Medical School gave women the opportunity to earn diplomas.) So Bremer suggested that Taussig instead study anatomy at a school that would give her credit for her work. She took his advice and enrolled at Boston University.

Taussig quickly dived into her studies and spent months working on an experiment supervised by her anatomy professor. The result was a paper describing her analysis of the heart tissue of various mammals. When a leading medical journal published her paper, Taussig was overjoyed. Not only was this an amazing feat for a student, it was also an extraordinary personal triumph for Taussig, who still struggled every day with her dyslexia.

Dr. Alexander Begg, the professor who had overseen Taussig's experiment, recognized her talent for medical research. He urged Taussig to transfer to the Johns Hopkins Medical School in Baltimore, Maryland, one of the country's premier medical schools. Taussig agreed and left for Baltimore in 1924, where she pursued her interest in *cardiology*, the study of the heart. Finally, three years later, she graduated with a medical degree.

Now a doctor, Taussig went to work in the Johns Hopkins heart clinic. While there, she met Dr. Edward Albert Park, who had been recently appointed professor and chairman of *pediatrics*, the department that specialized in the care of children. Park became a mentor to the new doctor and, in 1930, made Dr. Taussig an offer she

Dr. Edward Albert Park, head of the Johns Hopkins pediatric department, trusted Taussig, a recent medical-school graduate, to run a clinic.

couldn't refuse—to head his newly established pediatric heart clinic. Taussig gratefully accepted the position, as well as Dr. Park's challenge to learn everything she could about heart diseases, especially those found in newborn babies. She now knew her future lay in caring for children with heart problems.

At just about the time Taussig assumed her duties as head of the pediatric cardiology clinic, she began to notice that she was losing her hearing. She was horrified as the problem grew worse, but she refused to let a hearing loss interfere with her career. Taussig had dealt with adversity before in her life and she would do so again. She would find a way to practice medicine even if she became deaf.

Taussig began wearing a hearing aid that hung uncomfortably around her neck like a bulky necklace. Not satisfied, she taught herself lip reading to supplement her hearing. But she still had to figure out how to perceive the faint heartbeats of her tiny patients. Taussig experimented with a special stethoscope designed to amplify sound, but its usefulness was limited. Then she discovered a new way to listen—with her hands!

Dr. Taussig would first rest her fingertips on a child's chest. Then, by applying just the right degree of gentle pressure to the chest, she was able to detect the infant's heart pulsations. Taussig's colleagues marveled at what

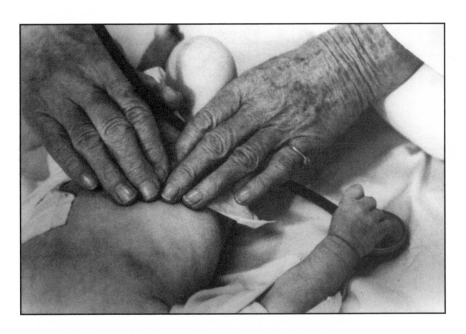

While her young patient grasps her stethoscope, Taussig examines the baby.

her fingers could perceive—such as abnormal heart rhythms—that they had missed with their stethoscopes.

Taussig searched tirelessly for a way to help *cyanotic* patients, infants with a lack of oxygen in their blood—a condition caused by several types heart defects. Infants with this problem are known as "blue babies," because the oxygen shortage makes their skin appear bluish in color. Taussig suspected that a narrowing of the *pulmonary artery*, which was responsible for carrying blood from the heart to the lungs, caused children to become cyanotic.

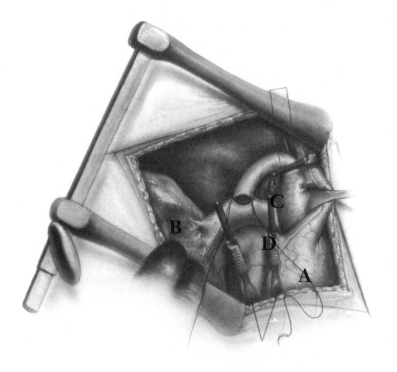

Taussig hoped to increase the flow of blood from the heart (A) to one of the lungs (B) by rerouting an artery from the aorta (C) so it could assist the narrowed pulmonary artery (D).

Taussig took her findings to Dr. Alfred Blalock (1899-1964), who developed the procedure to build an artificial vessel, or shunt.

To solve this problem, Taussig wanted to create a *shunt*—a passageway that would help increase the blood flow to a child's lungs. She shared her idea with Dr. Alfred Blalock, a famous surgeon on the Johns Hopkins staff. Blalock began experimenting in his laboratory, trying to find a way to make Dr. Taussig's idea work. Finally, he and another male surgeon, Dr. Vivien Thomas, operated on a live patient. They succeeded in attaching a smaller vessel to the pulmonary artery to increase the flow of blood to her lungs. The patient, a dog named Anna, lived for many years after the operation. Doctors Taussig and Blalock continued their experiments for two

Blalock and Dr. Vivien Thomas, his assistant, successfully implanted a shunt in this dog, Anna, whose portrait still hangs at Johns Hopkins.

more years while waiting for the chance to try their procedure on a human.

The breakthrough came one day in late November 1944, a month after the Johns Hopkins Hospital had admitted Eileen Saxon, a very sick child who was cyanotic. Eileen had been in and out of the hospital several times since her birth 15 months earlier. This time, the doctors did not expect her to live. Blalock and Taussig discussed

Eileen's situation. Given the child's grave prognosis for recovery, they decided to risk the new operation. Without the attempt little Eileen would surely die.

Everyone involved knew how important the operation could be for the many other children who suffered from similar heart defects. Dr. Blalock rose to the occasion and performed the procedure flawlessly as Dr. Taussig watched from the head of the operating table. The operation was a total success. When Eileen went home two months later, both Taussig and Blalock knew that surgeons everywhere could use the same operation to help other "blue babies."

News of the successful operation quickly reached the parents of other young cyanotic children, and new patients soon flooded Taussig's clinic. Physicians came also, eager to learn about the new Blalock-Taussig procedure. The technique spread rapidly around the globe, enabling countless sick children to survive infancy. (As a child outgrew the shunt, further surgery was often needed to ensure a healthy life.) One of the babies who underwent the operation grew up to become a concert pianist and dedicated a concert to Helen. Others who had married and raised families brought their children to see the woman who had given them back their lives.

Taussig's influence was felt outside the operating room as well. She trained others to become pediatric cardiologists, and those unable to study with her in person could read her book. First published in 1947, *Congenital*

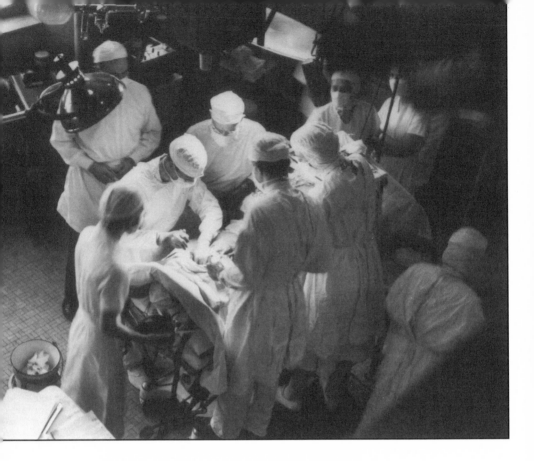

Blalock operates on a "blue baby" as Thomas (standing behind the hanging light) looks on in early 1947, a little more than two years after the first successful Blalock-Taussig operation.

Malformations of the Heart became a classic in the field. According to one university chief of cardiology, the book "provided the basis on which the discipline of pediatric cardiology was built." Not only that, he added, it provided "the stimulus that led many to enter the field of pediatric cardiology." Dr. Taussig, who as a teenager struggled just to be able to read, had revolutionized the study and treatment of heart disorders in children.

But Taussig's impact didn't end there. In 1962, a young German doctor and one of Dr. Taussig's former students brought her some horrible news from across the Atlantic Ocean. In Germany, doctors were baffled by a rare deformity called *phocomelia*. Instead of having normal arms or legs, babies born with phocomelia had flipperlike appendages. Some were even born with no arms or legs at all. Even worse, the number of babies with the deformity was on the rise for no known reason.

If she hoped to prevent phocomelia from attacking babies in America, Taussig knew she needed to learn more about what caused the condition. Traveling to Germany, she spoke with doctors frantically researching the problem. Taussig found that many of the women who later gave birth to deformed babies had used a sleeping pill called thalidomide. Even one dose taken by an unsuspecting woman in her first month of pregnancy could cause phocomelia.

Armed with this knowledge, Taussig returned to the United States to sound an alarm about the dangerous side effects of thalidomide. Since a number of countries marketed thalidomide under different names, she painstakingly researched and listed all the various trade names for the drug. A pharmaceutical company in the United States had applied to the Food and Drug Administration (FDA) for permission to market thalidomide under the name Kevadon. But thanks to Dr. Taussig's quick action, the FDA was able to stop

Kevadon's approval. The regulatory agency also warned the public to avoid the other trade names under which thalidomide was being sold in other countries.

Taussig's hectic pace finally slowed when she retired in 1963. She didn't consider retirement to be the beginning of a sedentary life, though. Having been promoted to full professor at Johns Hopkins in 1959—the first woman to attain that position—she continued to work there part time and to write articles for scientific journals. In 1965, Dr. Taussig became the first female president of the American Heart Association.

Following her retirement in 1963, Taussig underwent successful surgery to restore her hearing. But her deafness had not prevented her from rising to the top of her profession.

Throughout Taussig's long life, honors for her work poured in from many different sources. The one she valued the most came in 1964 when President Lyndon B. Johnson presented her with the Medal of Freedom, the highest award a president can give to an American civilian. As her citation stated, Taussig's "fundamental concepts have made possible the modern surgery of the heart which enables countless children to lead productive lives."

Helen Brooke Taussig's remarkably productive life came to an abrupt end on May 20, 1986, in an automobile accident—just four days shy of her eighty-eighth birthday. Many years earlier, she had counseled younger women doctors, "Whatever field you choose, just work quietly and steadily to make this world a better place to live and your life will be worthwhile." The value of Dr. Taussig's life can be seen in the thousands of people around the world who grew to become healthy adults as a result of her efforts.

Alma Dea Morani combined a love of sculpting and a fascination with medicine to become the first female member of the American Society of Plastic and Reconstructive Surgery.

6

Alma Dea Morani
The Hands of an Artist

*A*lma Morani's mother called her daughter "the worst tomboy on the street." Instead of playing with dolls and learning to sew like other girls her age, Alma ran around the neighborhood with the boys. This worried her mother, so for Christmas one year she gave her daughter a beautiful doll with long blonde curls and eyes that opened and closed. She hoped the doll would entice Alma away from the rough street games she played. The doll grabbed Alma's attention, all right, but not in the way her mother had expected. Transfixed by her doll's gaze, Alma recalled that she "cracked the head open to see how the eyes worked."

Young Alma possessed an inventive streak and an unquenchable thirst for knowledge. These traits, combined with her natural assertiveness and self-confidence, aided her immensely when she later became the first woman to practice in the demanding field of plastic surgery. Even though women had proved themselves as capable doctors by the 1920s, many people still considered surgery a man's job. But Alma never shied away from any challenge. "I'm going to do everything that boys can do," she vowed as a child, "only I have to do it better because I'm a girl."

Alma's parents were Italian immigrants from completely different backgrounds. Her father, Salvatore, was born to a lower-middle-class family in southern Italy. He made his living as a sculptor, as had his father and grandfather before him. Alma's mother, Amalia, was from the old and well-respected Gracci family. She loved to travel and had a passion for knowledge.

Shortly after their wedding, Salvatore received an important job offer to create religious sculptures in the United States. The opportunity was too good to pass up, so the couple packed their belongings and tearfully said their good-byes before making their way across the Atlantic Ocean to their new home.

Alma was born on March 21, 1907, on New York City's Lower East Side. This neighborhood was home to

Morani's parents were among the 15 million immigrants who poured into the United States between 1900 and 1915, accounting for almost one-third of the nation's population growth during this period.

many Italians and other new arrivals from eastern and southern Europe in the early 1900s. Many of the poor Italian immigrants lived in tiny, crowded apartments and struggled to make a living for their families. Amalia hated this situation and was homesick. She longed for the charm and elegance of her younger days. Knowing her husband could not leave his job, she returned to Italy with one-year-old Alma.

Alma and her mother stayed in Italy for the next three years. By the time they returned to the United States, little Alma could speak Italian. To her mother's relief, the family soon moved into a more comfortable neighborhood in the Bronx. More children followed for the Moranis, and Alma was now big sister to two younger sisters and a brother.

The idea of becoming a doctor took root early in Alma's mind. Her high-school biology teacher asked the class members to write a composition about what they wanted to be when they grew up. Unable to decide, Alma discussed her ideas with the instructor. After listening to Alma's interests, the teacher suggested medicine.

Alma seriously considered her biology teacher's advice. But whenever she mentioned that she wanted to study medicine, people always told her, "There are so few women doctors," or "That's a difficult career for a woman." Alma later remembered that those words only served as a challenge, "which, of course, made me decide that's exactly what I wanted to do."

A broken wrist erased any doubts she had about wanting to become a doctor. Horseback-riding was one of Alma's passions and she frequently gave riding lessons. Once, while teaching her two sisters to ride, she fell off her own horse and snapped her wrist. Alma's pain and fear seemed to disappear when she met the female doctor who treated her. Alma was fascinated. "I don't think I'd ever seen or heard of one before then," she exclaimed.

Suddenly, she realized that her dream was a real possibility. If this woman could become a doctor, Alma thought, then so could she.

In the mid-1920s, Alma began her premedical studies at New York University along with just seven other women. The vast majority of the class members were men, and the professors often treated the women as second-rate students. In chemistry class, for example, the professor segregated the women from the men. "And

A 1920s view of Washington Square, the heart of New York University

while we did our work as well as the men," remembered Alma, "we would be the last ones to be examined or the last ones to be quizzed."

After the unsupportive environment of her undergraduate program, Alma decided to attend an all-female medical school. She wanted to study medicine without being harassed or "talked down to" by men who felt she had no place alongside them. So, in autumn 1928, Alma entered the Woman's Medical College of Pennsylvania, the school from which Dr. Susan La Flesche Picotte had graduated in 1889.

Alma loved medical school. She found herself surrounded by other like-minded women who hoped to become doctors and by a predominantly female faculty who seemed genuinely interested in their students' goals. The students encouraged one another and drew inspiration from the women who had graduated before them.

But just as she was settling into her second year of studies, the stock market crashed in October 1929. The Great Depression had begun. As the economic situation worsened, Alma struggled to find enough money to pay her tuition. She had made it through the first year with money saved from her part-time job as a dental assistant in high school. During the second year, her parents helped her as best they could, but they couldn't afford much. To make ends meet, Alma tutored students in her anatomy and pathology classes. She persevered and managed to scrape by.

The more Alma learned about medicine, the more surgery captured her imagination. It was a hands-on way to "repair" people. But even though female doctors taught in most departments at Woman's Medical College, none performed surgery and surgery was taught only by men. Despite the school's generally supportive environment, students were not encouraged to pursue careers as surgeons. "The men were the surgeons," Alma recalled. "It never occurred to them that any women wanted to be surgeons." She couldn't resist the challenge.

After receiving her medical degree in 1931, Morani searched for a good hospital at which she could serve as a surgical intern. Internships for women were tough to come by, but luckily, through a friend of her father's, she gained acceptance into St. James Hospital in Newark, New Jersey. Morani was the first female to intern at St. James. Fortunately, the male surgical staff there helped the upstart Morani a great deal, inviting her to assist in their operations and giving her the valuable experience she needed.

In 1932, Dr. Morani returned to the Woman's Medical College of Pennsylvania as a surgeon. She worked with Dr. John Stewart Rodman, who had been her surgery professor when she had studied there. Although Rodman had not urged her to pursue surgery, he thought enough of her abilities to request her service as his assistant once she had completed her internship. As Rodman's assistant, Morani ran the outpatient surgery clinics. She also taught classes. On top of this grueling schedule, Morani was on call almost all the time for emergency surgical cases.

Among the cases she treated in the clinic were a large number of hand injuries. The challenge of repairing the injuries fascinated Morani "because it was sort of an artistic endeavor," a way to blend her appreciation of art acquired from her sculptor father with her love of surgery. She became convinced that the hospital should set up a clinic devoted specifically to taking care of such injuries. Morani boldly approached Dr. Rodman with the idea and, as a result, the first hand-surgery clinic in the city of Philadelphia opened at Woman's Medical College in 1935.

Working with hand injuries led Dr. Morani down another career path—reconstructive, or *plastic*, surgery. Morani's drift to plastic surgery made perfect sense given her talent for sculpting. She often spent her spare time crafting beautiful works of art, and plastic surgery seemed the perfect chance to use her surgical knife to make human flesh beautiful instead of simply leaving scars. So, in 1942, Alma decided to combine her two loves, surgery and art, and seek training in plastic surgery.

Even though she was by now a respected surgeon, Morani still found it difficult to get the plastic-surgery training she needed. She was able to attend only a short, one-month course at New York City's Polyclinic Hospital. Then, almost by chance, Morani found herself in 1946

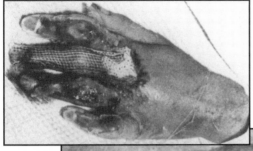

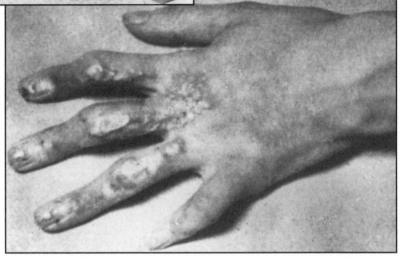

These pictures demonstrate how plastic surgery can help to reconstruct a mangled hand (left).

working with "one of the great men of plastic surgery"—Dr. J. Barret Brown of Barnes Hospital in St. Louis, Missouri.

Brown had not immediately welcomed the chance to work with Morani. He had no choice, however, because of an offer he had made to the Soroptimist Women's Club, a worldwide organization dedicated to creating educational and professional opportunities for women. The club had offered financial support to Dr. Brown for his work with war veterans, and out of gratitude for the club's help, he had asked if he could do anything for the members. Certainly, he did not expect their request—that Morani, herself a member, be allowed to study with him!

Even though Brown agreed to let Morani work with him for a year, she soon realized that he was not going to make the next 12 months easy for her. Dr. Brown allowed her to attend lectures and observe his operations, but he would not permit her to assist in the operating room. Nor did he include her in the postoperative meetings with his surgical team to discuss the results of operations.

After a few weeks of this treatment, Dr. Morani had had enough. Not wanting to waste her year of study by simply observing, she spoke to Brown privately. Her bold step produced a somewhat positive result: Brown allowed Morani to assist him in surgery on Saturdays when the male students were off for the weekend. The Saturday surgery load paled in comparison with the number of surgeries performed during the rest of the week, but Morani took advantage of every opportunity offered. By the end of her year with Dr. Brown, she felt she had gained a valuable education.

Finally, in July 1947, Dr. Morani was invited to join the American Society of Plastic and Reconstructive Surgery—the first woman to be so honored. It was a proud occasion that signaled the end of her training. She was now a plastic surgeon.

After her year with Brown, Dr. Morani returned to the Woman's Medical College of Pennsylvania. By then,

Dr. Kraeer Ferguson had replaced Dr. Rodman as the chief of general surgery. Morani approached Ferguson about establishing a separate plastic-surgery division within the general-surgery department. She could then pay full attention to the patients with specific reconstructive needs instead of dividing her time between general and plastic surgery. Ferguson, who Morani remembered as "another man who had little use for woman surgeons," bluntly refused her request. She was disappointed, but Morani took the refusal in stride and during the next few

The Woman's Medical College of Pennsylvania as it appeared when Morani returned in the late 1940s

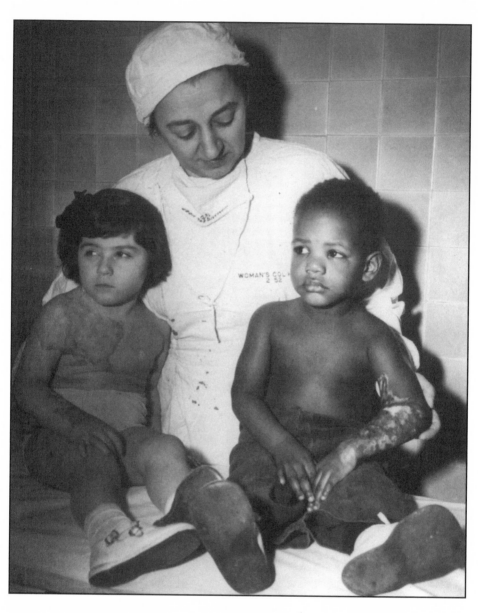

Throughout her long career, Dr. Alma Dea Morani never lost her love of working with patients. Here, in 1954, she examines two children in need of skin-grafting operations.

years methodically built a reputation as a respected plastic surgeon while also performing general surgeries.

When the Woman's Medical College finally appointed Morani professor of plastic surgery in 1955, she found she loved teaching because it gave her the opportunity to share her knowledge with others. Throughout the 1950s and 1960s, Alma continued to practice and teach. Over the years, she maintained an almost maternal relationship with her former students. "It's like having a group of children who have wandered around the world," she fondly explained.

Besides teaching and practicing medicine, Morani served as president of the Medical Women's International Association (MWIA) from 1972 to 1974. At the time, members of the MWIA included more than 12,000 female physicians from countries spanning the globe. Dr. Morani came up with a project that would take advantage of the abilities of these doctors to help others. Under her guidance, the MWIA would hold a conference for the Family Planning International Assistance group (FPIA) for the purpose of educating female physicians from the Far East in modern methods of family planning.

Dr. Morani set about carefully organizing the event, realizing that if the conference was successful "it would be a credit to women doctors around the world." Female physicians from 17 countries—including Indonesia, Malaysia, Taiwan, and Egypt—soon gathered in the city of Manila in the Philippines. There they heard lectures detailing the most up-to-date information on family planning. The doctors took the new knowledge back to their own countries to incorporate into their practices. The event proved to be an overwhelming success.

In her role as president of MWIA, Alma Morani traveled constantly, meeting associates in many other countries. Through friends in Taiwan she received an exciting new opportunity. The Taiwanese National Defense Medical Center was setting up a plastic-surgery department. Doctors there asked Morani to teach for two months in Taipei, Taiwan's capital.

Morani found the offer intriguing and eagerly accepted. The two months she spent on the island nation off the coast of China were packed with surgeries and lectures. Morani and her three Taiwanese assistants succeeded in establishing a well-organized department of plastic surgery. That stay would be the first of several trips to Taiwan for the "Orchid Lady," as her new friends came to call Morani.

During these years, Dr. Morani continued to develop as an artist. The same hands that painstakingly repaired the human body also created beautiful sculptures. Children were her favorite subject to sculpt. Art even enhanced Morani's surgical skills because her creations, she explained, helped her to "see the possibilities of correcting deformities." Before operating, Dr. Morani would make a sculpture of her desired results to give herself a "definite plan to follow."

Along with her own sculptures, Morani avidly collected the artwork of others. Over 400 pieces, created by both Morani and other artists, are displayed in the Morani Art Gallery that opened in 1985 at the Medical College of Pennsylvania (formerly the Woman's Medical College). After retiring from medicine, Morani remained involved with the gallery. Because of her conviction that plastic surgery and sculpture "help each other," she introduced art courses into the curriculum at the Medical College of Pennsylvania. Other medical schools throughout the country have since followed suit.

Dr. Alma Morani refused to listen when people tried to persuade her not to become a plastic surgeon. Her work has been a blessing to hundreds of patients, as well as an inspiration to generations of young medical students hoping to enter the demanding world of surgery. Young women especially can learn from Alma's success. You have to say to yourself, she counseled them, "I can do it as well as a man because I have the knowledge and capability. A man in my position would not do it any different or any better." Judging from Dr. Morani's accomplishments, none have.

Along with raising millions of dollars for research into the cause and prevention of birth defects, Virginia Apgar (1909-1974) devised a revolutionary method to quickly evaluate the health of newborn infants.

7

Virginia Apgar
The Highest Score

*E*ven before the newborn baby begins to cry, the delivery-room nurse has set two timers, one for one minute and the other for five minutes. As each timer goes off, the nurse performs a brief series of checks—called "Apgars"—that are designed to evaluate the infant's general condition at birth. Within minutes after birth, the newborn's heart rate, respiration, muscle tone, reflex, and color are checked and recorded, and the exhausted mother is cuddling her new baby with the confidence that her child appears to be in good health.

For the series of checks that evaluated her baby's condition twice in its first minutes of life, the new mother can thank Dr. Virginia Apgar. Dr. Apgar developed the Apgar Score System in 1952 when she realized doctors and nurses needed a quick testing system in the delivery room. Since then, countless people have lived healthy lives because respiratory disorders or other problems that they experienced at birth were immediately diagnosed and treated.

But there's more to Virginia's legacy than her revolutionary scoring system. Fresh from medical school in the mid-1930s, the doctor broke ground in the new medical field of *anesthesiology*—the study and application of drugs that cause a loss of sensation. In later years, while head of the National Foundation-March of Dimes, Apgar raised millions of dollars for research into the cause and prevention of birth defects. Throughout her life, she pursued her interests with passion, conquered challenges with creativity, and sprinkled everything she did with a liberal dash of humor.

Born in Westfield, New Jersey, on June 7, 1909, Virginia was the second child and only daughter of Charles and Helen Apgar. According to Virginia, hers was a family that "never sat down." Her father, an insurance executive, was fascinated with the mysteries of astronomy and wireless telegraphy, including the new development of radio technology. Charles Apgar was also a musician, and the family's living room constantly

Virginia Apgar with her older brother, Lawrence

resounded with strains of music from his impromptu concerts. Young Virginia shared her father's enthusiasm for music.

In school, Virginia proved to be the kind of well-rounded student teachers dream about. Not only did she excel inside the classroom, but she was also a star on the Westfield High School track team. During her high-school years, Virginia took great pleasure in her science classes, and she developed an obsession with medicine that never left her.

In 1925, the young high-school graduate entered Mount Holyoke College in South Hadley, Massachusetts, where she devoted herself to studying science. *Zoology*, the study of animals and how they live, was especially intriguing to Virginia, so she concentrated her coursework on that subject. Chemistry and anatomy also piqued her curiosity and found a place in her schedule.

Apgar (seated at left) poses with other students on the Mount Holyoke campus, the oldest women's college in the United States.

Although her studies alone would have overwhelmed most students, Virginia found time to join seven varsity athletic teams, act in dramatic productions, report for the college newspaper, and play the violin in the school's orchestra. She managed all this while supporting herself by working in the college library and waiting tables. Apgar left Mount Holyoke in 1929, degree in hand, anxious to leap the next hurdle in her education—Columbia University College of Physicians and Surgeons in New York City. The scholar, athlete, and waitress was well on her way to becoming a doctor as well.

One of the few women in her class at medical school, Apgar was again a top student, graduating with honors in 1933. Intending to become a surgeon, she embarked on a highly prestigious internship in surgery at nearby Columbia-Presbyterian Medical Center. For two years she worked feverishly, studying surgery and participating in as many as 200 operations.

But Dr. Apgar would not fulfill her dream of becoming a surgeon. Instead, she eventually concluded that earning a living as a surgeon would be almost impossible for her because most patients in the 1930s still preferred to be operated on by men. In any case, Apgar's interests had begun to drift toward the growing field of anesthesiology. *Anesthetics* are drugs that cause a loss of sensation or induce unconsciousness so that patients can undergo operations without pain. The challenge of administering these drugs appealed to the young doctor.

Prior to Apgar's time, nurses had administered anesthetics. But as surgery grew in complexity, specialists slowly took over the work. Apgar felt it was time for pioneering research in the field, so in 1935 she gave up surgery to concentrate on anesthesiology. Little did Apgar know she was embarking on a career that would forever change the way doctors around the world handled babies in the delivery room.

Dr. Apgar began her studies under the experienced nurse-anesthetists at Columbia. She then traveled to the University of Wisconsin to train under Ralph M. Waters,

In the mid-1930s, Apgar studied under Professor Ralph M. Waters, one of the United States' foremost scholars in the field of anesthesiology.

founder of the nation's first academic program in anesthesiology and future president of the American Board of Anesthesiology. Finally, Apgar worked at New York City's Bellevue Hospital with another renowned anesthesiologist, Emery A. Rovenstine. Dr. Apgar finally became a board-certified anesthesiologist in 1937.

In 1936, even before she was fully certified, Apgar began teaching anesthesiology at Columbia-Presbyterian. Two years later, she was promoted to the position of assistant professor. Columbia-Presbyterian appointed her to direct its division of anesthesiology later in 1938, making Dr. Apgar the first woman to head a department at the highly respected university hospital.

In her 11 years as a department head, Apgar helped anesthesiology grow into an outstanding academic program. Believing that anesthesiology should be a separate specialty with its own highly trained experts, she handpicked the best physician-anesthesiologists to teach new doctors and medical students. Columbia University showed its appreciation of Apgar's innovations by promoting her to full professor in 1949—the first woman on Columbia's medical faculty to hold that position.

When she accepted her new post, Apgar gave up her other duties as department head so she could spend all of her time studying the use of anesthetics in childbirth. Having observed thousands of births throughout her years as an anesthesiologist, she knew that an infant's initial minutes of life were crucial to his or her survival. Apgar

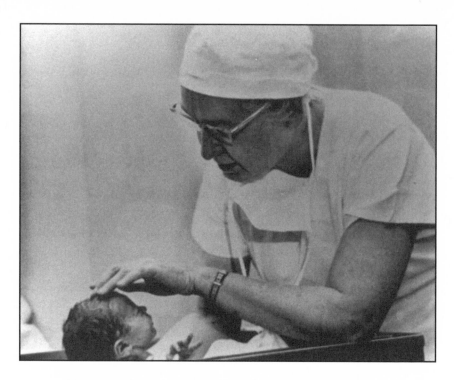

Apgar checks the condition of a newborn moments after delivery. Recognizing the need for a quick testing procedure, Apgar developed her simple scoring system that is still widely used today.

believed that doctors needed an efficient system to evaluate a newborn's condition. Her solution was a simple yet revolutionary scoring system that quickly became popular with delivery-room personnel.

Using the name **APGAR** as an acronym to make the system easy to remember, nurses would check a new baby for five vital signs: **A**ppearance, or color; **P**ulse, or heart rate; **G**rimace, or reflex; **A**ctivity, or muscle tone; and **R**espiration. Doctors would give the baby a numbered score from 0 to 2 for each vital sign and then add the individual scores, hoping for a total between 8 and 10. A score between 5 and 7 signaled that the baby needed medical attention without delay. This treatment might involve nothing more than holding oxygen under the newborn's nose for a few minutes to increase the oxygen supply in the blood. After five minutes, the doctor or nurse performed the checks again to ensure that the baby's Apgar score had increased to 8 or above.

The Apgar Score System			
Score	**0**	**1**	**2**
Appearance or color	Blue or pale	Body pink; hands and feet blue	Completely pink
Pulse or heart rate	Absent	Less than 100 beats per minute	More than 100 beats per minute
Grimace or reflex	Absent	Grimace	Grimace and cough or sneeze
Activity or muscle tone	Limp	Some flexing of arms and legs	Active motion
Respiration	Absent	Slow, irregular; weak cry	Good; strong cry

The Apgar Score System was announced in 1952 and earned Dr. Virginia Apgar instant recognition and praise throughout the medical community. Its use spread quickly to hospitals around the United States and in many other countries. Soon, numerous babies around the world were being evaluated by Apgar's ingenious system.

As the years passed, Apgar became even more committed to maternal and infant health. In 1959, at the age of 49, she took time off from her job at Columbia to earn a master's degree in public health from the Johns Hopkins University. Instead of returning to Columbia when she finished, Apgar accepted a position with the National Foundation-March of Dimes as director of research on birth defects and *anomalies*, or conditions that differ from what doctors consider to be normal.

Dr. Apgar devoted the remainder of her life to increasing worldwide public support for research into the cause, prevention, and treatment of birth defects. Characteristically, she juggled a busy schedule with the March of Dimes, first becoming head of the division studying *congenital deformities*—physical impairments that exist at birth—then director of research, and, finally, senior vice-president for medical affairs.

Remarkably, Apgar held other positions in the late 1960s while working at the March of Dimes. She served Cornell University Medical College in New York City as both a lecturer and professor of pediatrics. In 1973, the Johns Hopkins School of Public Health hired Apgar to lecture in its genetics department. As in her hectic days as a student at Mount Holyoke College, Apgar was never happier than when she was spending every moment of her time constructively.

While working for the National Foundation-March of Dimes, Apgar knew she had to convince the public that making donations would help to prevent birth defects. With the energy of a much younger woman, Apgar traveled around the world to educate people about the prevention of birth defects. Her hard work paid off. When she first arrived at the March of Dimes, its annual income through donations and grants totaled $19 million. Thanks to Apgar's monumental efforts, the funds had risen to $46 million by 1974.

In addition to her passion for research, Dr. Apgar loved to teach. Her sense of humor and an unusual teaching style made her popular with her students. For instance, her medical students learned the anatomy of the spinal column by feeling Dr. Apgar's own unusually large *coccyx*, or tailbone. Her passion for teaching could also be seen in her medical practice. To better explain to parents how birth defects originated, she carried a tiny preserved fetus in a bottle in her purse.

Apgar's desire to help the public understand birth defects prompted her to write *Is My Baby All Right?* in 1972. Her book described for parents the possible medical problems that babies can have before, during, and after birth. It also provided instruction in the prevention of birth defects and informed parents of infants with birth defects how to get help.

When she wasn't working, Apgar spent her time pursuing such assorted hobbies as music, fishing, golf, and stamp collecting. She even made her own stringed instruments, a talent she had been perfecting since her student days at New York's Columbia-Presbyterian Medical Center. Apgar had been resourceful in getting parts for her instruments back then. One day, she stole a wooden shelf from a telephone booth because it was "just right" for part of a viola she was making.

In recognition of her powerful impact as a teacher, physician, and leader in the prevention of birth defects, Dr. Virginia Apgar garnered a host of awards. In 1973, the alumni association of the Columbia University College of Physicians and Surgeons gave Apgar the Gold Medal for Distinguished Achievement in Medicine, making her the first woman to receive the honor. An award from the American Society of Anesthesiology quickly followed. The *Ladies' Home Journal*, a popular women's magazine, named her 1973's "Woman of the Year in Science and Research."

The year after receiving these accolades, Virginia Apgar succumbed to liver disease on August 7. She was only 65. All her life she had been a maverick, unafraid to chart new territory. Apgar left behind her volumes of research on birth defects and a delivery-room system that continues to save the lives of newborns. She spent her life

Apgar being honored as 1973's "Woman of the Year in Science and Research"

fulfilling a vow she had once made while explaining why she carried in her handbag medical tools necessary to perform a *tracheotomy*, a procedure to open the airway when someone cannot breath: "Nobody, but nobody," she had declared, "is going to stop breathing on me."

Despite having few role models, Dorothy Lavinia Brown rose to become the first black female surgeon in the South and a Tennessee state legislator.

8

Dorothy Lavinia Brown
Beating the Odds

*D*orothy stared out her bedroom window. The staff at the orphanage was kind, but the little girl still longed for a family of her own. The orphanage in Troy, New York, was the only home nine-year-old Dorothy had ever known, having been placed there by her mother when she was just five months old.

None of the people who walked up to the visitors' desk ever asked to see her. Maybe it was because she was one of the few black children in the orphanage of a mostly white town. Whatever the reason, Dorothy decided to change the situation. She told the superintendent she wanted to have visitors, just like the other children. Her straightforward approach worked. A few days later, Mr. and Mrs. Frank Coffeen stopped at the visitors' desk and requested to see Dorothy.

From this early experience, Dorothy learned the value of assertiveness. If she had not spoken up for herself, she would have continued to spend visitors' days alone, standing at the window and watching the world go by. But now the Coffeens were *her* special visitors, and she looked forward enthusiastically to visitors' day.

Dorothy's forthrightness and determination helped her to become the first black female surgeon in the U.S. South. In later years, her sense of purpose would also lead her into the political arena.

Dorothy Lavinia Brown's story began on January 7, 1919, when a young woman gave birth to a baby girl in Philadelphia, Pennsylvania. The unmarried mother moved with her baby to Troy, New York. Unfortunately, she was unable to raise her daughter alone. When Dorothy was just five months old, her mother placed her in the Troy orphanage, where the young girl would live for the next 13 years.

Dorothy excelled as a student while at the orphanage. Her grades regularly earned her the yearly prize awarded to good students, but she was not studying just to win prizes. Dorothy had a much bigger goal in mind— she wanted to become a doctor.

The orphanage in Troy, New York, where young Dorothy Lavinia Brown grew up after her mother realized she could not take care of her

Dorothy had known she wanted to be a doctor ever since she underwent a tonsillectomy when she was five years old. While most children would have been afraid to have an operation to remove their tonsils, the little girl loved the experience. Everything at the hospital fascinated Dorothy: the bright lights, the friendly nurses, the doctors with half of their faces hidden behind mysterious masks. Dorothy watched everything the doctors did with a keen eye. By the time she recovered from her surgery, she knew she wanted to be a doctor too.

Luckily, young Dorothy didn't realize the odds were stacked against her. "Somebody," she laughed, recalling her early life, "should have had the sense to say to me, 'You can't do it because you're black, you're a woman and you're poor.'" Fortunately, no one ever did. From the age of five, everything Dorothy did with her life led to the day she proudly accepted her medical degree.

Just after Dorothy turned 13, her mother arrived at the orphanage to collect her daughter. Up to that time, the orphanage had been Dorothy's whole life, and her mother was not even a distant memory. The sudden change in her life upset and confused Dorothy, and she ran away from her mother's home four times. At last, her mother realized they had spent too many years apart for a familial bond to develop. She placed her daughter in the home of the Jarrett family in Albany, New York, as a domestic servant, one of the few jobs available to African American girls in the 1930s.

Dorothy knew that becoming a doctor required an expensive education, so she saved every penny of her meager earnings as a servant. During her free time, Dorothy began her medical education by reading books from the Jarretts' large collection. She consumed works on Latin, algebra, and chemistry. Finally, after a year and a half in Albany, she had saved almost $500 and was prepared to return to Troy to finish high school.

One obstacle immediately threatened to block her path: she had no place to live in Troy. But when the high school's principal discovered her predicament, he contacted a couple who agreed to let her stay in their home. The couple, Samuel and Lola Redmon, grew to love their young boarder. Even after Dorothy's money ran out, they shared their home with her and made her their foster daughter. At last, Dorothy had a family.

As she settled into a stable life with the Redmons, Dorothy found time to explore other interests. She loved to draw, and for a time her foster parents and teachers encouraged her to develop her artistic talents instead of dreaming about medicine. But Dorothy never wavered in her desire to become a doctor.

In high school, Dorothy developed a fondness for music and played the double bass violin in the school orchestra. Throughout her life, many stressful moments would melt away as Dorothy relaxed to the peaceful strains of classical music.

Following her high-school graduation, the next step toward a medical degree was college. Again, circumstances forced Dorothy to work to earn money for her education. Her efforts brought her to the attention of a Methodist women's group in Troy that helped qualified young people obtain scholarships. With their assistance, Dorothy received the money she needed to study at Bennett College, a small Methodist school in Greensboro, North Carolina.

Like her foster parents and her teachers at Troy High School, Dorothy's advisors at Bennett tried to steer her away from a career in medicine. She should go into teaching instead, they told her. Again Dorothy insisted on following her heart. She enrolled and excelled in the science courses she knew would prepare her for medical school. The woman who remembers growing up "at a time when people said black kids couldn't learn because they're dull and stupid" graduated second in her class in 1941, one step closer to a medical degree.

Dorothy's march faltered about half a year after her graduation when the United States plunged into World War II. By 1942, the nation was shipping men overseas in ever-increasing numbers to fight, leaving a vacuum of prime job openings for women to rush into, especially women with backgrounds in science. Dorothy's preparation for medical school won her a good job. For nine months, she worked as a civilian employee of the Army Ordnance Department in Rochester, New York, inspecting ammunition targeted for overseas delivery.

Dorothy Brown's job had a lot of responsibility. Realizing that few African Americans held similar positions, Brown began to appreciate the importance of being a role model. She resolved that when she became a doctor—as she was still sure she would—she would speak to other people about her work. She hoped she could inspire others to achieve their goals as well.

As 1944 rolled by, Brown took stock of the money she had saved to continue her education. The sum fell short of what she needed, but timely financial assistance

Like these women working on the noses of fighter planes for Douglas Aircraft in 1943, Dorothy Brown took advantage of new job opportunities opened up by World War II.

from the same Methodist women's group that had earlier secured her scholarship to Bennett enabled Brown to apply to medical school. She won acceptance into both Howard University in Washington, D.C., and Meharry Medical College in Nashville, Tennessee, the only two African American medical schools in the United States.

Ever practical, Brown chose Meharry because she could live more economically in Nashville than in Washington. The young medical student made the most of her opportunity while at the Tennessee school. Finally, in 1948, after more than two decades of dogged determination, Dorothy Brown graduated in the upper third of her class at Meharry Medical College.

Having won the battle to become a doctor, Brown followed up with a year-long internship at New York City's Harlem Hospital, the same hospital at which May Edward Chinn had earlier trained. But she soon grew restless for an even greater challenge and applied for a spot in Harlem Hospital's surgical residency program. (A *residency* is a period of specialized training for new doctors—in Brown's case, training in surgery.) Brown was not surprised that the hospital declined her application.

Meharry Medical College, organized in 1876 as part of Central Tennessee College, became an independent school in 1915.

"We were still in a time when it was very unpopular and almost impossible for a woman to get a surgical residency," she explained.

But just as Dorothy Brown knew when she was 5 years old that she would become a doctor, she knew at 30 that she was destined to become a surgeon. She went back to Meharry Medical College and pleaded with the chief surgeon, Dr. Matthew Walker, to allow her to complete a residency at Meharry.

Walker was torn. He believed Brown could handle the work, but the male doctors in the surgical residency program wanted no women in their midst. Finally, in spite of the opposition, Walker gave Dorothy her chance and admitted her into the residency program. "Dr. Matthew Walker was a brave man," Brown said, acknowledging the pressure that Walker was under not to accept her. Since Dr. Walker stood by her, Brown vowed, "I was definitely not going to fail."

She never did. For five years, Dr. Dorothy Brown worked so hard at Meharry that her colleagues began calling her "Mule Brown." Like a stubborn mule, she refused to budge from her chosen path, never believing, as many people did at the time, that surgery was too difficult for women.

After completing her residency at Meharry Medical College in 1954, Brown became the first black woman to work as a surgeon in the South. She poured all her energies into her new job at Meharry's George W. Hubbard

Dr. Matthew Walker had made it possible for Dorothy Brown to get training as a surgeon when he ignored the protests of his male staff and admitted her to Meharry's surgical residency program.

Hospital, perfecting her surgical skills and teaching medical students. Meharry was impressed with her dedication and appointed the tireless Brown assistant professor of surgery. Later, Dr. Brown took on the additional responsibility of director of student health services.

In addition to her duties at Meharry, Brown practiced medicine at nearby Riverside Hospital in Nashville. In 1959, less than six years after completing her surgical residency, Riverside appointed her chief of surgery. She had reached the zenith of her medical career.

But Brown didn't stop there. Thinking back to her own lack of role models when she was younger, the chief

142

surgeon took a special interest in the interns and residents at both the Meharry and Riverside hospitals. She guided them as they assisted her with operations—teaching them how to make proper diagnoses, training them in surgical techniques, and showing them how to monitor

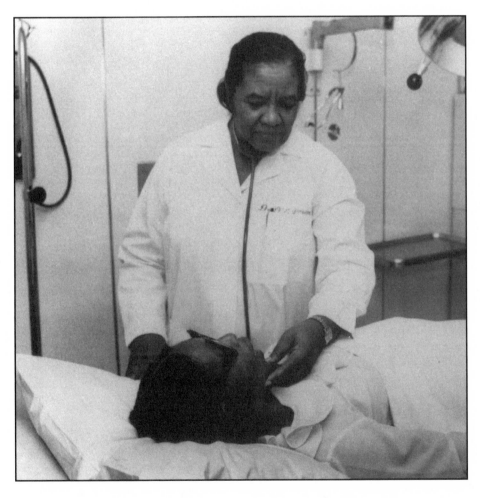

Brown examines a patient at Meharry's George W. Hubbard Hospital.

patients during the crucial recovery period. Dr. Brown remained in her capacity as educational director and chief of surgery at Riverside until the hospital closed its doors in 1983.

With her demanding responsibilities and hectic pace, Brown enjoyed only rare moments of time off for herself. Nonetheless, she dreamed of squeezing one more special responsibility into her life—a child of her own. Still single on her fortieth birthday, Brown considered adoption. But no unmarried woman had ever adopted a child in the state of Tennessee.

Her opportunity came when a single, pregnant woman offered Brown the chance to adopt her baby when it was born. The doctor checked into the state's laws and realized that nothing prevented the adoption. Another "first" thus took place when Brown joyfully took her new daughter home. She named the baby girl Lola Redmon after her own beloved foster mother.

In 1966, Brown set her sights on yet another challenge—running for political office. While no black woman had ever been elected to the lower house of the Tennessee State Legislature, Brown was not intimidated. Anybody, she felt, could succeed with "the motivation and will to do what [they] want to do." "Mule Brown" had the will, and the voters of Tennessee's fifth district rewarded her tenacity by electing her to a two-year term.

As a state representative, Dorothy wrote and sponsored a bill to liberalize the state's abortion law. Abortion

The Tennessee State Capitol, where Brown served an occasionally controversial term as a state legislator

was illegal in Tennessee at the time, and Dr. Brown's bill would have permitted abortion for victims of rape and incest. The response to her effort was anything but positive. "You would have thought I'd opened the gates of hell," an astonished Brown gasped.

Not surprisingly, her bill died a quick death. But before her term expired, Brown succeeded in promoting a bill that led to the establishment of Negro History Week in Tennessee. Efforts like hers led to the later creation of Black History Month. Believing that knowledge would lead to racial tolerance, Brown explained, "If you know people and you know where they come from and you know their difficulties and you know what their lives are like, then you may not fall in love with those people, but you'll never be able to hate them again."

As testament to the inspiration that people have drawn from Dorothy's triumphs through the years, many diverse groups, from religious and political organizations to scientific and medical associations, frequently ask her to talk about her life and the challenges she faced while becoming a doctor. She especially treasures her talks with children. You are responsible for making your own dreams come true, Brown tells them, and she offers herself as living proof that anything is possible.

With honorary degrees in humanities from North Carolina's Bennett College and Cumberland University in Tennessee, a term in the Tennessee State Legislature, and almost five decades of medical experience, Dr. Brown has surpassed most of her goals. Still, she looks forward to each new day and any new challenge. She continues her private medical practice, teaches surgery at Meharry Medical College, and serves as a general surgeon at Hubbard Hospital.

The journey from the Troy orphanage to medical prominence was long and difficult, but Dorothy Brown's motivation, will, and genuine love for people sustained her through even the darkest times. She remains a beacon of hope for all people who carry impossible dreams of their own inside their hearts.

A Timeline of Women in Medicine

c. 2500 B.C.: Merit Ptah of Egypt is the first known woman doctor.

1490-1470 B.C.: Women in Egypt attend medical school.

Sixth Century B.C.: Greek women practice as healers.

Fifth Century B.C.: Women attend Greek physician Hippocrates's medical school.

Fourth Century B.C.: Athenian female doctor Agnodice narrowly escapes execution for practicing medicine.

A.D. First Century: European women work as physicians, midwives, and nurses.

Fourth Century: Early Christian female deaconesses heal the sick.

390: In Rome, Fabiola builds the first Christian hospital.

533: The religious order of deaconesses is abolished.

Sixth Century: Queen Radegonde founds a hospital in Poitiers, France, and also opens a hospice for lepers.

758: Empress Komyo founds the first documented hospital in Japan.

Eleventh Century: Physician Trotula teaches and practices medicine in Italy. Her written works, including *Diseases of Women*, remained popular for hundreds of years.

Eleventh Century: The University of Salerno begins to have many female medical graduates, several of whom go on to write books on medicine; the university was open to women for several centuries.

Twelfth Century: The Beguine order of nuns is founded; the Beguines established hospitals across northern Europe in the following centuries.

Twelfth Century: Hildegard of Bingen, a Benedictine abbess, writes several books on medicine and science.

1220: The University of Paris prohibits women from practicing medicine.

1250: Hersend, a woman, becomes physician to King Louis IX of France.

1322: Parisian Jacoba Felice is excommunicated from the Roman Catholic Church for being a woman doctor.

mid-1300s: Cecilia of Oxford is surgeon to Queen Philippa of England.

1390: Dorotea Bocchi becomes chair of medicine at the University of Bologna in Italy, a position she will hold for 40 years.

1422-1423: Costanza Calenda graduates from the University of Naples in Italy as a woman doctor.

1487: Queen Isabella of Spain pioneers the military field hospital to care for soldiers in the Crusades against the Moslems.

1609: French midwife Louise Bourgeois publishes an influential book covering problems of infertility, pregnancy, childbirth, and infant mortality.

1754: Dorothea Erxleben becomes Germany's first woman to graduate from a medical school.

January 23, 1849: Elizabeth Blackwell becomes the first woman to earn a medical degree in the United States.

1853-1856: Florence Nightingale becomes a legend nursing soldiers during the Crimean War.

1857: Blackwell, her younger sister Emily, and Maria E. Zakrzewska open the New York Infirmary for Women and Children, the first hospital in the world directed by women doctors.

1859: About 300 women in the U.S. have earned medical degrees.

January 1864: Mary Edwards Walker achieves official status in the U.S. Army as an assistant surgeon with the 52nd Ohio Regiment.

1865: President Andrew Johnson presents **Walker** with a Congressional Medal of Honor for her valor during the Civil War.

1868: In France, women are allowed to enter medical degree programs.

1868: Emily Stowe becomes the first woman doctor in Canada.

1871: Blackwell helps to establish the National Health Society in England to educate people about hygiene.

1872: Russia begins admitting women into its medical schools.

1873: Elizabeth Garrett Anderson becomes the first female member of the British Medical Association.

1873: The American Medical Association admits its first woman member, Sarah Stevenson.

1889: Susan La Flesche Picotte becomes the first American Indian woman to graduate from medical school.

1891: Portugal gains its first woman doctor, Amelia Cardia.

1900: There are about 5,000 women doctors in the U.S.

1913: In Walthill, Nebraska, **La Flesche Picotte** opens the first hospital on the Omaha reservation.

1915: The American Women's Medical Association is founded by physician Bertha Van Hoosen.

1919: The Medical Women's International Association is founded by U.S. physician Esther Lovejoy.

1921: Five percent of U.S. medical students are women.

1926: **May Edward Chinn** becomes the first black woman to receive a medical degree from Bellevue Hospital Medical College.

1936: Lya Imber becomes Venezuela's first woman doctor.

1941-1945: When World War II forces many U.S. men out of medical school to fight overseas, more women are allowed into the schools.

November 1944: The first cyanotic baby is saved using a procedure developed by **Helen Brooke Taussig**.

1947: **Taussig's** book, *Congenital Malformations of the Heart*, is published and soon becomes a standard text in cardiology.

July 1947: **Alma Morani** becomes the first woman to join the American Society of Plastic and Reconstructive Surgery.

1947: Gerty Radnitz Cori becomes the first U.S. woman to win the Nobel Prize for physiology or medicine.

1952: **Virginia Apgar** invents APGAR, a scoring system used to evaluate a newborn baby's vital signs.

1954: **Dorothy Lavinia Brown** becomes the first black woman to work as a surgeon in the South.

1957: **Chinn** is presented an honorary citation for her work in cancer research by the New York City Cancer Committee of the American Cancer Society.

1962: Women make up six percent of all U.S. doctors.

1964: The American Pediatric Society elects its first woman president, Hattie Alexander.

1964: **Taussig** receives the Medal of Freedom from President Lyndon B. Johnson.

1965: The American Heart Association elects **Taussig** as its first woman president.

1970: A larger number of women gain entrance to medical schools in response to a successful complaint filed by the Women's Equity Action League against every medical school in the United States.

1972-1974: **Morani** serves as president of the Medical Women's International Association.

1973: **Apgar** becomes the first woman to receive the Gold Medal for Distinguished Achievement in Medicine from Columbia University.

1973: 70 percent of all doctors in the Soviet Union are women.

1976: Women are 29.5 percent of all doctors in Finland and 17 percent of Thailand's doctors.

1980: American women earn approximately 33 percent of all medical degrees in the U.S.

1983: 40 percent of Romania's doctors are women.

1995: 20.7 percent of all U.S. doctors are women.

1997: Dr. Nancy W. Dickey becomes the first woman elected president of the American Medical Association.

Bibliography

Anderson, Bonnie S., and Judith P. Zinsser. *A History of Their Own: Women in Europe from Prehistory to the Present.* 2 vols. New York: Harper & Row, 1988.

Baldwin, Joyce. *To Heal the Heart of a Child.* New York: Walker, 1992.

Beard, Charles A., ed. *A Century of Progress.* New York: Harper & Brothers, 1933.

Beatty, William K., and Geoffrey Marks. *Women in White.* New York: Scribner, 1972.

Bennett, Lisa. "Women Doctors Are Changing the Face of Medicine." *American Health*, April 1996, 72-75.

Blackwell, Elizabeth. *Pioneer Work in Opening the Medical Profession to Women.* New York: Schocken, 1977.

Bonner, Thomas Neville. *To the Ends of the Earth: Women's Search for Education in Medicine.* Cambridge: Harvard University Press, 1992.

Brooke, Elisabeth. *Medicine Women: A Pictorial History of Women Healers.* Wheaton, Ill.: Quest Books, 1997.

Brown, Marion Marsh. *Homeward the Arrow's Flight.* Nashville: Abingdon, 1980.

Chinn, May Edward. "An Autobiography." Manuscripts, Archives, and Rare Books Division. Schomburg Center for Research in Black Culture. New York Public Library, New York.

Fenichel, Carol Hansen, Regina Markell Morantz, and Cynthia Stodola Pomerleau, eds. *In Her Own Words: Oral Histories of Women Physicians.* New Haven: Yale University Press, 1982.

Ferris, Jeri. *Native American Doctor: The Story of Susan LaFlesche Picotte.* Minneapolis: Carolrhoda, 1991.

Filler, Louis. Biographical sketch of Dr. Mary E. Walker. Special Collections. Syracuse University Library, Syracuse, N.Y.

Garrison, Fielding H. *An Introduction to the History of Medicine*, 3rd ed. Philadelphia: W. B. Saunders, 1922.

Golemba, Beverly E. *Lesser-Known Women: A Biographical Dictionary*. Boulder, Colo.: Lynne Rienner, 1992.

Green, Carol Hurd, and Barbara Sicherman, eds. *Notable American Women: The Modern Period, a Biographical Dictionary*. Cambridge: The Belknap Press of Harvard University Press, 1980.

Hurd-Mead, Kate Campbell. *Medical Women of America*. New York: Froeben, 1933.

James, Edward T., ed. *Notable American Women: 1607-1950, a Biographical Dictionary*. Cambridge: The Belknap Press of Harvard University Press, 1971.

La Flesche Family Papers. Nebraska State Historical Society, Lincoln, Nebr.

Leonard, Elizabeth D. *Yankee Women: Gender Battles in the Civil War*. New York: W. W. Norton, 1994.

Lopate, Carol. *Women in Medicine*. Baltimore: The Johns Hopkins University Press, 1968.

McHenry, Robert, ed. *Famous American Women: A Biographical Dictionary from Colonial Times to the Present*. New York: Dover, 1993.

Miller, Ronnie. "Dorothy Brown: Strong Will Overcomes Obstacles to Career." *Nashville Banner*, July 28, 1986.

Neill, Catherine A. "Helen Brooke Taussig." *The Journal of Pediatrics* 125 (1994): 499-502.

Olsen, Kirsten. *Chronology of Women's History*. Westport, Conn.: Greenwood, 1994.

Peale, Norman Vincent. *Power of the Plus Factor*. Old Tappan, N.J.: Fleming H. Revell, 1987.

Ploski, Harry A., and James Williams, eds. *The Negro Almanac: A Reference Work on the Afro-American*, 4th ed. New York: John Wiley & Sons, 1983.

Read, Phyllis J., and Bernard L. Witlieb. *The Book of Women's Firsts*. New York: Random, 1992.

Ross, Ishbel. *Child of Destiny: The Life Story of the First Woman Doctor*. London: Victor Gollancz, 1950.

Smith, Jessie Carney, ed. *Notable Black American Women*. Detroit: Gale Research, 1992.

Snyder, Charles McCool. *Dr. Mary Walker: The Little Lady in Pants*. New York: Arno, 1974.

Stein, Leon, ed. *Lives to Remember*. New York: Arno, 1974.

Telgen, Diane, and Jim Kamp, eds. *Notable Hispanic American Women*, 1st ed. Detroit: Gale Research, 1993.

Uglow, Jennifer S., ed. *The International Dictionary of Women's Biography*. New York: Continuum, 1982.

Wilson, Dorothy Clarke. *Bright Eyes: The Story of Susan La Flesche Picotte, an Omaha Indian*. New York: McGraw-Hill, 1974.

"Women in Medicine, 1995 Data Source." American Medical Association brochure. Chicago: American Medical Association, Women in Medicine Services, 1995.

Interviews with the Author:

Brown, Dorothy Lavinia. Telephone interview by author. Personal notes. May 23, 1996.

Morani, Alma Dea. Telephone interview by author. Personal notes. May 24, 1996.

Index

ABOUT THE AUTHOR

JACQUELINE KENT was born and raised on a Jamaican sugar plantation. After graduating from the University of Miami in Florida, she served five years as an officer in the U.S. Air Force. Kent, who lives with her husband and baby daughter, is now working on her master's degree in Latin American history and gender studies at the University of Nevada at Reno.

Photo Credits
Photographs courtesy of: front cover, pp. 12, 14, 18, 25, 30, 63, 77, 82, 86, 92, 95, 100, 102, 113, 124, National Library of Medicine; p. 6, Rick Wacha; pp. 9 (both), 21, 22, 31, 38, 41, 46, 53, 55, 58, 105, Library of Congress; p. 17, American Medical Association; p. 27, The Boston Medical Library in the Francis A. Countway Library of Medicine, Boston; p. 33, Sophia Smith Collection, Smith College, Northampton, Mass.; pp. 35, 79, 111 (both), Dittrick Museum of Medical History; pp. 43, 50, 139, National Archives; p. 51, Massachusetts Commandery Military Order of the Loyal Legion and the U.S. Army Military History Institute; pp. 56, 67, 69, Nebraska State Historical Society; p. 72, May Edward Chinn Photograph Collection, Schomburg Center for Research in Black Culture; pp. 74, 76, Special Collections, Milbank Memorial Library, Teachers College, Columbia University; p. 84, Joe Pineiro, Columbia University; pp. 89, 96, 98, The Alan Mason Chesney Medical Archives, The Johns Hopkins University; p. 93, © 1981 TADDER/Baltimore; p. 94, Ranice W. Crosby, The Alan Mason Chesney Medical Archives, The Johns Hopkins University; p. 107, New York University Archives; p. 114, Archives and Special Collections, Medical College of Pennsylvania Collection, Allegheny University of the Health Sciences; pp. 118, 121, 122, 126, 131, The Mount Holyoke College Archives and Special Collections; pp. 132, 140, 142, 143, Meharry Medical College Archives; p. 135, Collection of the Rensselaer County Historical Society, Troy, N.Y.; p. 145, Tennessee State Capitol.